The Writer's Room
Unleashing Your Inner Storyteller

A Masterclass in Crafting
and
Publishing Your Story

By:
Betsy Chasse

The Writers Room - A Masterclass in Crafting and Publishing Your Story

Publisher: Rampant Feline Media/Betsy Chasse www.betsychasse.net

© 2024 All Rights Reserved

ISBN Paperback: 979-8-9910714-4-4
ISBN EBook: 979-8-9910714-5-1

Praise for Betsy Chasse

Catherine Stilo, Mastermind Member

"I love the process that Betsy guides us through in our Master Mind group. It's forcing me to dig deeper, ask tougher questions, and face things I may have skirted over had I been writing alone. The process is also becoming a beautiful container for greater inspiration to flow. I remember moments and events I had forgotten and want to include them in the story! Thank you so much, Betsy, for the expertise, love, and support. You provide a perfect balance of honest feedback and cheerleading as I move through raw vulnerability toward authentic expression." -

Fonda Taylor- Screenwriting

Without the Betsy Chasse writing class, I would never have accomplished this TV Pilot and story bible. Selected in 4 competitions and won Best Feature at the Berlin Indie Film Festival--all within six months of finishing her class. A huge debt of gratitude to my writing coach!

Kerry Jehanne-Guadalupe - Author

I admire Betsy's ability to listen beyond words; she's been instrumental in guiding both myself and others I know toward profound self-discovery through our writing. With this gift, Betsy is excellent at assisting aspiring writers on their path to publication and enhancing the skills of established authors to refine their craft further.

Taylor Boone - Novel and Documentary

Betsy's coaching has been nothing short of transformative, catalyzing profound shifts in my creative journey. Her guidance has empowered me to overcome internal obstacles and ignited fresh and innovative perspectives, fundamentally reshaping my creative projects.

Table of Contents

Part 1:
The Craft of Writing 8

    Introduction: The Journey of a Writer 9
    Why Writing Matters 9
    My friend BoB 10
    The Writer's Mindset 11
    How did I find the writer in me? 12
    A little bit about AI 13

Chapter 1
Fiction vs. Non-Fiction 14

    Understanding the Differences 14
    Choosing Your Path: Fiction or Non-Fiction 14
    The Different Types of Memoirs 15
    Hybrid Writing: When Genres Overlap 16
    The 5 W's - Understanding Your Reader: Demographics and Psychographics .. 16

Chapter 2
Storytelling Fundamentals 22

    Building Blocks of a Compelling Story 23
    Character Development 23
    Tools: Character Breakdown Worksheet: 25
    Plot Structure and Pacing 28
    The Hero's Journey and Other Story Structures 29
    Tools: The Hero's Journey Map and Worksheet 31
    Case Studies for the different types of story structures – Three Act Structure, Freytag's Pyramid, The Seven Point Structure 38
    Setting and World-Building (for Fiction) 45
    Dreamwork for Storytelling 46
    Creating a Beat Sheet and Chapter Outline 50

Chapter 3

Crafting Non-Fiction Narratives 55

The Art of Research: Methods, Using Quotes and Annotations, Fair Use...... 55

The Role of Narrative in Non-Fiction.................................... 59

Using Personal Experience in Non-Fiction and Finding Your Voice.......... 59

Chapter 4

Writing Techniques 63

Mastering Dialogue 64

Show vs. Tell 65

Using Descriptive Writing... 65

Writing with Authenticity 67

Developing Your Voice 67

Forward, Preface, and Introduction 68

Chapter 5

Overcoming Writer's Block 73

Common Causes of Writer's Block 73

Practical Strategies for Breaking Through.............................. 74

Sustaining Creativity and Motivation................................... 75

Part 2:

Polishing Your Manuscript 77

Chapter 6

The Art of Revision 79

AI and other editing and writing tools 80

Working with Beta Readers.. 82

Receiving and Working with Feedback – Self-Editing 83

Chapter 7

Professional Editing... 86

Types of Editing: Developmental, Copyediting, Proofreading............ 86

How to Find and Work with an Editor 88

  Example of Editorial Services Agreement.................89
  Common Pitfalls to Avoid..........................92

Part 3:
Getting Published...................................94
Chapter 8
Choosing Between Self-Publishing and Traditional Publishing.....95
Chapter 9
Traditional Publishing 98
  Understanding the Traditional Publishing Process 98
  How to Find and Approach Literary Agents................99
  Crafting a Winning Book Proposal (for Non-Fiction) 100
  Navigating Contracts and Rights 101
  What Does a Basic Publishing Agreement Look Like?......101
  What are the types of rights publishers are seeking? ..102

Chapter 10
Working with a Publisher 104
  The Role of an Editor in Traditional Publishing 104
  Marketing and Promotion: What to Expect 104
  Understanding Royalties and Advances 105

Part 4:
Self-Publishing: The Truth about Self-Publishing 109
Chapter 11
The Self-Publishing Revolution 113
  Pros and Cons of Self-Publishing........................113
  Choosing the Right Platform 114
  Ebooks vs. Print: Formats and Considerations 116
  Monitoring Sales.......................................118

Chapter 12

Preparing for Self-Publishing ... 120
ISBNs, Barcodes ... 120
Cover and Interior Design ... 122
Formatting Your Book for Different Platforms ... 132
Setting the Right Price ... 138

Chapter 13

Marketing Your Book ... 140
Building an Author Platform ... 140
Social Media Strategies ... 148
Estimated Marketing Budget ... 151
When to Launch ... 152

Chapter 14

Distribution and Sales ... 155
Best-Seller Campaigns and General Sales ... 156
Getting Your Book into Bookstores and Libraries ... 156
Maximizing Online Sales – marketing channels ... 157
Leveraging Reviews and Reader Feedback ... 158

Part 5:

Beyond the Book ... 160

Chapter 15

Legal and Financial Considerations ... 161
Copyrights and Trademarks ... 161
Taxes and Accounting for Writers ... 163
Setting Up a Writing Business ... 164

A Little Betsy Note ... 166

Appendices ... 167
Writing Resources and Tools ... 167
Sample Query Letters and Book Proposals ... 169

Recommended Reading List ... 175

Part 1:
The Craft of Writing

Introduction: The Journey of a Writer

Why Writing Matters

Storytelling is the oldest form of entertainment and the most ancient tool for sharing our traditions, culture, and experiences with future generations. Since man could express themselves through imagery and words, we have shared our wisdom about anything and everything. Where the bison are, what creatures and plants we found, what tastes good, and what makes you sick! Who begat who, tales of great battles, who won, who lost? We created songs, poetry, and stories of wild adventures to share our history, entertain us, and bring us hope. Stories, especially if told well, evoke strong emotions of sadness, fear, and, more importantly, hope, inspiration, and love.

Through its power, storytelling can transform perceptions, influence experiences, and profoundly impact lives. It can also support personal growth and heal the body, mind, and soul.

Good storytelling does all this and more. This is why I write.

Your story matters and deserves to be told. Even if you decide to write a book simply to give to your children and friends, trust me when I tell you that when you finish your book, you will be a different person than when you started.

Many of my clients come to me with the belief that "I'm not a writer" or "I'm not good enough." I invite you to let that belief go. Some people are indeed born with a knack for putting pen to paper; for some, it takes work. That's ok, do the job. Later in this book, I will share ways you can work through any hidden beliefs about writing, working with writing coaches and tools available to support your process. Start by reminding yourself that any doubts and fears about writing are just silly little thought monsters needing to be banished. Don't get caught thinking about "Will my book be successful?" or "Will anyone read it?" That doesn't matter. What matters is your commitment to yourself to write your book.

Everything I share in this book applies to both fiction and nonfiction writing. For my nonfiction writers, Readers are not looking for a guru to dictate solutions but seek connection, relatability, and authenticity. They want to feel safe and engaged as they read. In nonfiction writing, creating a space for readers to connect with your message is crucial. Personal anecdotes and storytelling can effectively weave your insights into the narrative, keeping readers engaged.

My approach to writing is universal and applicable to any genre or subject. It is intuitive and rooted in a deep understanding of readers' and characters' emotional and psychological dimensions. For nonfiction writers, this principle extends to real people, including yourself. Adhering to this approach can significantly enhance how your work is received.

This is the process I use and have shared with hundreds of writers, from best-selling authors to novice storytellers. It has proven effective, and I am excited to share it.

This book is a comprehensive process, beginning with the moment the idea for a book strikes your heart and mind through publishing. It may feel overwhelming at first. I advise you to take it step by step. Read the whole book first to have a vision for the process, then use it as a reference tool as you move through each writing phase.

While I developed this process, tips, and tools over my 35 years of writing and filmmaking, some of the definitions used in this book are pulled from multiple sources, including AI/ChatGPT, Merriam-Webster dictionary, Dictionary.com, and Cambridge Dictionary. I will provide a list of other references at the end of the book.

My friend *BoB*

A unique part of my writing process is that I believe that any creative idea that comes to me isn't entirely mine. It's a co-creation brought forth through me. Some might call this inspiration from God, The Universe, or Spirit Guides; I call it BoB.

Over the years, I have developed a deep connection to BoB, and I trust that together, we can and do bring forth creative ideas, books, films, essays, and blogs that someone in this reality needs, especially me.

Every creative project I embark upon is a journey with all the highs and lows life offers. Since the innovative idea isn't entirely mine, and I am simply a steward, I respect that it has a life of its own. To that end, I often have to shut up, listen to it, and allow it to have its journey.

What does that mean? Sometimes, an idea for the project might be something I don't like, but it's right for the project. In short, I have to get my ego out of it. There is a saying in writing… sometimes you have to kill your babies… rough, I know…however, sometimes I get attached to an idea simply because it's mine, and when that happens, BoB will step in and in one way or another, make sure that I let go and let BoB (the project) evolve the way it should and not necessarily the way my ego wants it to.

I have conversations with Bob; I ask, "What do you think of this?" and listen to the answer. When we get out of the way, our more profound connection to our creative spirit will support the process.

So, don't be afraid to be a little weird with it. Be open to what comes up, and be willing to try out ideas that maybe don't sit right with you at first. If it's not meant to be, you will know it.

Practice learning to tell the difference between your ego wanting to be correct, your attachment to an idea, and the idea evolving into what it is destined to become.

The Writer's Mindset

Many people wonder why they should write a book. They say things like "I'm not a writer" or "No one cares about my story." So, before we dig in, I want you to let those limiting beliefs go. You are a writer and learning the skills to improve: your story and voice matter.

There are several reasons why writing a book is essential. For instance, writing a memoir can be one of the most powerful, transformative, and healing experiences ever. By sharing your story, you can also give the world a unique perspective that only comes from you and your experience. The world needs more people sharing their authentic and vulnerable stories, especially now.

Writing a book is also a great way to market and publicize yourself. It helps people learn more about you and your work, builds brand awareness, and creates marketing and publicity opportunities you might not currently have available.

However, many people struggle to finish their books. They may have been working on it for years and still have not completed it. The reason for this may not be what you think. It is not necessarily fear holding you back but rather a lack of understanding of how to write a good story. Even if you know how to tell a good story, there is a specific structure to writing a successful book. Story structure is the foundation for any good fiction or non-fiction book.

Think of building a house. You can't paint the walls and hang the curtains until you lay the foundation. Similarly, you can't write a good book until you have a solid outline. While it may not be the most exciting part of writing, it's essential to be organized and plan before you start writing. By doing so, you'll create space for your creativity to flow. You'll see you're opening up a new world of ideas and possibilities when you follow what I teach.

Before we start writing your book, I want you to write down the answers to these questions. This will become your book's mission statement. It is the most important conversation you must have with yourself before starting.

Why are you writing this book?
What do you hope to achieve by writing this book?
Are you committed to writing this book? How committed are you?
What are you willing to let go of to write this book?

Now, the first piece of writing you will do is write out your answers to create a mission statement for yourself and your book. Hang it on your wall or carry it in your bag. But have it available so that when you waver, you can read it and remind yourself why you're doing this.

Forgive me for sounding a bit woo-woo. When we fully commit to something, we move energy towards that outcome. If you think of anyone who has ever achieved incredible success or even completed something they initially didn't know they could. The first step in the process was committing to it, no matter what. This is your commitment to yourself and your book.

You are about to embark on a fantastic journey. It will be exhilarating, frustrating, and scary, and you will experience all the feels.

And I hate to ruin the ending for you….

But it's all going to be ok.

Commit yourself to completing as much of the process as you can. Remember, you don't have to publish; you don't have to do any of this. This is your choice, and you must promise yourself first.

How did I find the writer in me?

For the first 30 years, I did not believe I could be a writer. While I was intelligent and capable and had made a successful career in the film business, my job was on the more practical side of creating media. I did budgets and organized shoots, etc. When asked to help make What The Bleep Do We Know?!, I realized that the original script needed a complete rewrite and was challenged to do it. That worked out well! I was lucky to work with another writer and thrilled to find that I indeed was creative, and my ideas weren't bad ideas that no one would want to read. My first screenplay and writing credit ended up becoming a major box-office success. Even after that, I still held onto the doubt about my skills.

One day, a few years later, something harrowing forced me to sit down and put pen to paper. It was the only way I could find to process the hurt of the experience. By accident, I was asked to publish my little book of essays as a practice run for a client publishing her book- this was in the early days of self-publishing (ok, it wasn't THAT long ago!) I never expected anything to come of the book – Metanoia – A Transformative Change of Heart. I didn't even market the book. It was supposed to be a simple test of the process. After selling six thousand copies of that book a year later, I received my first book deal with Atria/Simon and Shuster and wrote Tipping Sacred Cows.

I can't promise you a book deal or success; not everything I write is "successful." The most valuable thing from my experience is that I found something I truly loved to do. I found something that allows me to heal my heart when it hurts and to share my lessons learned; I am blessed to make a living doing and, most importantly, a new belief about myself. I can if I put my mind to it.

I felt so proud of myself for completing my first book. That feeling will never leave me, even if nothing else ever happened with writing. I will always have that, and you will, too.

A little bit about AI

Before we get started, let's talk a little bit about AI and writing.

People have a lot of opinions about AI. People are scared of AI. I get it.

For full disclosure, I used AI to help me write this book. [GASP!]

With that being said, AI did not write this book.

AI is a great tool. In this book, I will share places where it can be helpful.

For this book, AI helped offer definitions and easy-to-follow explanations for topics like Freytag's Pyramid. I know what this is; I have explained it many times. So, I typed out my quick definition but asked AI to help me write it to clarify and ensure I didn't miss anything. I also checked other references to ensure all was as it should be. Correctness is essential when explaining these concepts.

I used AI to help me create case studies and examples of how different techniques are used. For instance, when I reviewed how different story structures can be used, I asked AI to help me. I knew which book used which type of structure and could easily explain it, but I asked AI to do it for clarity and, honestly, time-saving. I then reviewed what AI gave me, edited it further, and corrected it when needed because AI doesn't always get it right…

I DO NOT use AI to write *FOR* me. And neither should you. Unless you're writing an instruction manual, and even then, make sure that AI got the red and blue wires right; otherwise, there will be problems.

Sometimes, AI is handy when looking for a word or phrase. I also use Google for these types of queries.

No one person can know everything, and using reference tools like AI can and will help you become a better writer. But they are tools, not replacements for your words or your way of telling the story.

AI can be sexy and make things seem more manageable and faster. But the people reading your book deserve to hear your voice, your version. And you deserve to be heard.

Now, Let's get started!

Chapter 1
Fiction vs. Non-Fiction

Understanding the Differences

At its core, writing can be divided into two broad categories: fiction and nonfiction. While both forms aim to communicate ideas, entertain, and provoke thought, they do so in fundamentally different ways.

Fiction is a creative form of writing in which the author invents characters, settings, and plots. However, actual events may inspire the stories; they are, at heart, the product of the writer's imagination. Fiction allows writers to explore "what if" scenarios, create worlds and beings that do not exist in reality, and delve into the minds and emotions of their characters. It's a form of artistic expression that offers endless possibilities, limited only by the writer's creativity.

Nonfiction, on the other hand, is grounded in reality. It deals with facts, actual events, and real people. Nonfiction writers must adhere to the truth, presenting information accurately and reliably. This genre includes a wide range of writing, from biographies and memoirs to essays, journalistic articles, and academic papers. The goal of nonfiction is often to inform, persuade, or educate the reader about a particular subject or event.

Understanding the differences between these two forms is crucial for any writer. It affects how you approach your writing and connect with your audience.

Choosing Your Path: Fiction or Non-Fiction

Deciding whether to write fiction or non-fiction is one of the most significant choices a writer can make. This decision will shape the direction of your work and influence the techniques you use to tell your story.

If you're drawn to storytelling, the art of character creation, and the freedom to invent, fiction might be the right path for you. Fiction offers the opportunity to explore ideas and themes in a way that is not bound by the constraints of reality. It's a space where you can let your imagination run wild and where the only limits are those you set for yourself.

On the other hand, non-fiction could be your calling if you're passionate about real-world issues, fascinated by true stories, or have a deep desire to inform and educate. Writing non-fiction requires a commitment to accuracy and a responsibility to present information truthfully. It often involves research, interviews, and a deep understanding of your subject matter.

Consider your strengths, interests, and the type of stories you want to tell. Reflect on what excites you as a writer and where your passions lie. Whether you choose fiction or non-fiction, writing authentically and staying true to your voice is critical.

The Different Types of Memoirs

Memoirs are a unique form of non-fiction that allows writers to share their personal experiences and insights with the world. Unlike autobiographies, which cover a person's life, memoirs focus on specific moments, themes, or periods in the writer's life.

There are several types of memoirs, each offering a different perspective:

1. **The Traditional Memoir:** This type of memoir follows a straightforward, chronological narrative. It often covers a significant period in the author's life and is focused on personal growth, overcoming challenges, or exploring a particular theme.

2. **The Thematic Memoir:** Instead of focusing on a specific period, a thematic memoir revolves around a central theme or idea. This could be anything from love, loss, or identity to a passion for a particular hobby or profession. The narrative might jump around in time, connecting different experiences through the central theme.

3. **The Confessional Memoir:** In a confessional memoir, the author shares intimate, often painful experiences with brutal honesty. These memoirs can be cathartic for the writer and powerful for the reader, offering insight into the human condition and the **complexities of life.**

4. **The Portrait Memoir:** This type of memoir focuses on the author's relationship with another person, often a parent, child, mentor, or friend. The narrative explores the impact of this relationship on the author's life and personal development.

Understanding the different types of memoirs can help you determine the best way to tell your story. Whether you're recounting a transformative experience or exploring a particular theme, the structure and focus of your memoir will play a crucial role in how it resonates with readers. It's ok if your memoir doesn't fit perfectly into one of the categories. Your memoir can encompass more than one; hybrids happen.

Hybrid Writing: When Genres Overlap

The boundaries between fiction and non-fiction are becoming increasingly blurred in modern literature. Hybrid writing, which combines elements of both genres, is gaining popularity as writers experiment with form and content.

Hybrid writing can take many forms:

- **Creative Nonfiction:** This style uses literary techniques often associated with fiction—such as character development, dialogue, and vivid descriptions—to tell a true story. Creative nonfiction allows writers to explore the emotional truth of their experiences, offering a more engaging and immersive reading experience.

- **Faction:** This is a blend of fact and fiction, where the writer incorporates fictional elements into a narrative based on actual events. This approach can fill in gaps in historical records or explore "what if" scenarios based on actual occurrences.

- **Autofiction:** Autofiction combines autobiography and fiction, allowing writers to explore their lives through a fictionalized lens. The author blurs the lines between reality and imagination in autofiction, creating a personal and universal narrative.

Hybrid writing offers a unique opportunity to push the boundaries of traditional genres. It allows writers to experiment with form, play with narrative structure, and explore new ways of storytelling. However, it also requires a careful balance, ensuring that the blend of fact and fiction is transparent to the reader and that the story's integrity is maintained.

Regardless of your choice, the process for writing your book remains the same. I prefer the hybrid model for the works I publish. Even my novel, Killing Buddha, was based on a true story (mine). It allowed me to share the wisdom I have learned fun and engagingly without naming names, shifting timelines and events, combining characters and events to suit a narrative, and achieving my goal of sharing wisdom without being preachy or teaching.

The 5 W's - Understanding Your Reader: Demographics and Psychographics

I have an idea for a book – now what?

Okay, the muse has hit! You've got an idea for a book you'd like to write and have decided on your style, so where do you start?

Get to know your reader. Understand your genre and explore other books that might be similar. Take the time to learn who your readers are and why they might read your book.

You are not writing in a vacuum. I suspect you are writing so others will read your book, so why not consider them while writing?

When an idea for a book strikes, it can be an exhilarating experience. However, to turn that initial spark into a fully developed story, a few critical questions are crucial to writing a compelling book; I call them the 5 W's—Who, What, When, Where, and Why. These questions help shape the story and ensure the book resonates with its intended audience.

This is the psychographics of your reader. Psychographics are very different from demographics.

Think of it like this:

Demographics:

- Definition: Demographics refer to statistical data that describes the quantifiable characteristics of a population.

- **Focus:** This data focuses on who your audience is measurably.

- **Common Demographic Data:**
    - Age
    - Gender
    - Income level
    - Education level
    - Occupation
    - Marital status
    - Ethnicity
    - Geographic location
    - Family size

- **Use Case:** Demographics help identify people's essential characteristics, making segmenting and targeting audiences based on these traits easier. For example, a company might target products to women aged 25-35 in urban areas with a specific income level.

Psychographics:

- **Definition:** Psychographics delve into a population's qualitative characteristics, focusing on attitudes, interests, values, and lifestyles.

- **Focus:** This data focuses on why your audience behaves as they do, revealing their motivations, beliefs, and emotional triggers.

- **Common Psychographic Data:**
    - Personality traits
    - Values and beliefs
    - Hobbies and interests
    - Lifestyle choices
    - Attitudes and opinions
    - Social status and affiliations
    - Buying behaviors and motivations

- **Use Case:** Psychographics help create a deeper understanding of what drives and motivates an audience, allowing for more personalized and emotionally resonant messaging. For example, a brand might market eco-friendly products to consumers who value sustainability and are firmly committed to environmental causes.

Combining Demographics and Psychographics:

Understanding demographics and psychographics is essential for creating a complete profile of your target audience. While demographics provide the basic framework of who your audience is, psychographics reveal the inner motivations and preferences that drive their behaviors, allowing for more effective communication and engagement strategies.

Why does this matter? Unlike the "old days," when typically, boys between the ages of 7 and 16 were really into skateboards or even dinosaurs, nowadays, anyone at any age could have continued their love of those things into adulthood or vice versa. Nowadays, you might find a tween interested in quantum physics!

Of course, writing for tweens, young boys, vs. young girls may require a different tone or style. If you've answered the 5 W's, you will clearly understand who you are writing for and why.

I've had clients who thought they were writing for only one group and found a new group of potential readers, expanding their book in ways they had not imagined.

The 5 W's:

Pro Tip: Get nerdy, go deep, and leave no stone unturned.

Who: Identifying the Ideal Reader

The first question is, "Who is the ideal reader for this book?" Understanding your target audience is essential for crafting a story that connects with readers deeply.

- **Interests:** Consider what topics, themes, or genres your ideal reader is passionate about. Are they drawn to mysteries, romance, self-help, or historical fiction? Knowing their interests helps you tailor the content to meet their expectations.

- **Struggles:** Identify the common challenges or pain points your reader faces. What problems are they trying to solve? What fears or insecurities do they wrestle with? By addressing these struggles in your book, you create a sense of empathy and relevance.

- **Dreams:** Finally, consider the aspirations and desires of your ideal reader. What do they hope to achieve or experience? Whether personal growth, career success, or finding love, your book can guide or inspire them to pursue their dreams.

By clearly defining your reader, you create a roadmap for your writing. This understanding shapes not only the content but also the tone, style, and even the pacing of your book.

What: Understanding the Reader's Needs

Next, ask, "What do they want, need, or desire from reading this book?" This question digs into the specific outcomes your reader is seeking.

- **Wants:** What is the reader hoping to gain from your book? It could be entertainment, knowledge, insight, or even comfort. Identifying their desires helps you deliver a story that meets their expectations.

- **Needs:** What underlying needs does your book address? Perhaps your reader needs to escape from the stress of daily life, or they need guidance during a challenging time. Understanding these needs allows you to provide value beyond the surface level.

- **Desires:** Beyond practical needs, what deeper desires does your reader have? Do they long for adventure, connection, or self-discovery? Tapping into these desires can make your book more compelling and emotionally resonant.

By answering the "What," you ensure that your book provides meaningful content that fulfills the reader's desires and needs, making it more likely to leave a lasting impact.

Why: Motivations Behind the Reader's Choice

The third question, "Why do they want it?" is about uncovering the motivations behind the reader's decision to pick up your book.

- **Emotional Drivers:** What emotions are driving your reader's choice? Are they seeking hope, healing, excitement, or inspiration? Understanding these emotional drivers allows you to craft a narrative that resonates personally.

- **Intellectual Curiosity:** Perhaps your reader is driven by a desire to learn or understand something new. What questions are they trying to answer? What knowledge gaps are they hoping to fill? Addressing their curiosity can make your book intellectually satisfying.

- **Social Influence:** Consider the external factors that might influence your reader's decision. Are they looking for a popular book in their social circle, or do recommendations from trusted sources influence them? Understanding these influences can help you position your book effectively in the market.

The "Why" helps you connect with the deeper reasons behind a reader's choice, ensuring that your book aligns with their motivations and encourages them to engage fully with the content.

When: Timing the Reader's Needs

Timing is everything, which leads us to the question of "When do they want it, and when do they need it most?"

- **Life Events:** Consider the significant life events that might drive a reader to seek out your book. Are they going through a transition, such as a career change, a breakup, or a move to a new city? Your book could offer the guidance or comfort they need during these pivotal moments.

- **Seasonal Needs:** Consider the time of year when your book might be most relevant. For example, a self-improvement book might be popular when readers set resolutions at the start of a new year, while a light-hearted romance might be a summer favorite.

- **Emotional Timing:** Beyond specific events, consider when your reader might be emotionally ready to engage with your book. Are they at a point where they're seeking transformation, or are they simply needing an escape? Understanding this timing helps you craft a narrative that meets them where they are.

Answering the "When" ensures that your book is timely and relevant, increasing the likelihood that it will resonate with readers when needed.

Where: Context of the Reader's Life

Finally, ask, "Where do they want or need this book?" This question helps you understand the context in which your reader will engage with your book.

- **Business:** If your book is aimed at professionals, where will it be most valuable in their work lives? Perhaps they need leadership strategies, advice on navigating corporate culture, or inspiration for innovation.

- **Home**: If your book is more personal, consider where it fits into the reader's home life. Is it a resource for parenting, a guide for managing household finances, or a story that brings comfort at the end of a long day?

- **Relationships**: Perhaps your book is focused on relationships. Where does it provide the most value? Is it about improving communication with a partner, understanding family dynamics, or building stronger friendships?

- **Personal Growth:** For books aimed at personal development, consider where your reader is on their journey. Are they at the beginning stages of self-discovery, or are they seeking advanced strategies for growth and transformation?

By considering the "Where," you ensure that your book fits seamlessly into the reader's life, providing value in the context that matters most to them.

Developing a connection with your reader is crucial to becoming a compelling storyteller. Writing is not just about expressing oneself; it's also about ensuring that the reader understands and can relate to the story. Knowing how your audience perceives information is essential as a public speaker or someone who works with clients. This doesn't mean you must compromise your writing style, but understanding your audience and their interests will help you convey the story more effectively.

By answering these 5 W's, you create a clear, focused vision for your book that is deeply connected to the needs and desires of your target audience. This framework guides your writing process and enhances your story's relevance and impact, making it more likely to resonate with readers and succeed in the marketplace.

Believe it or not, doing this exercise first will reveal new ideas that will improve your book. You will find nuances, unique elements, and story opportunities you didn't know existed.

Chapter 2
Storytelling Fundamentals

At the heart of every great story lies a combination of essential elements that captivate the reader. These building blocks include characters, plot, setting, and theme. When these elements are thoughtfully crafted and interwoven, they create an engaging and memorable narrative.

This is important regardless of your book type- Fiction or Non-Fiction. Have you ever watched a good documentary? Believe it or not, they told you a story, even if the story is the journey of a tiny cell.

Here's an example:

Meet Celia, a single, determined cell nestled within the lining of a human gut, where she lives a quiet life, absorbing nutrients and dividing to maintain the body's delicate balance. One day, a sudden wave of invading bacteria storms the gut, threatening to disrupt everything she knows. As chaos erupts, Celia must quickly adapt, using every ounce of her energy and genetic programming to fend off the intruders. Alongside her fellow cells, she forms alliances with immune cells, learning to recognize friends from foes. Through this crisis, Celia evolves, growing more robust and resilient and developing new receptors that make her better equipped for future battles. What started as an ordinary life cycle became an epic journey of survival, transformation, and renewal. Celia's experience makes her a vital defender in the body's ever-changing landscape.

Now that was fun and interesting, wasn't it?

Here's the exact explanation without using storytelling:

A cell in the human gut, such as an epithelial cell, plays a role in absorbing nutrients and maintaining the lining of the intestine. When bacteria enter the gut, these cells must respond by activating their defense mechanisms, including signaling the immune system and reinforcing their structural barriers. The cell may develop new receptors to recognize and respond to threats more effectively. This process helps the cell and the surrounding tissue protect the body from infection and maintain overall health. Over time, the cell adapts to resist future invasions and supports its functions within the gut environment.

OK- SUPER BORING! (at least for me!)

Before diving into storytelling's building blocks, here's a tip for non-fiction writers: Remember that your book has characters, even if they aren't people. It also has a plot, whether it's the journey of a cell from one place to another or the exploration from one point of knowledge to another. Your story includes a theme, such as personal growth, healing, or expanding one's understanding of a subject. And it has a setting, whether in a business environment, a personal context, or elsewhere. Keep these elements in mind as you review this section.

Building Blocks of a Compelling Story

1. **Characters**: The people or beings who populate your story. They should be complex, relatable, and capable of growth. Readers should care about what happens to them.

2. **Plot**: The sequence of events that make up your story. A compelling plot should have a clear beginning, middle, and end, with rising tension leading to a climax and resolution.

3. **Setting**: The world in which your story takes place. This includes the time, place, and atmosphere. A well-developed setting can enhance the mood and tone of your story.

4. **Theme**: The underlying message or central idea of your story. It gives the narrative depth and often reflects universal truths about the human experience.

Understanding and mastering these building blocks is essential for any storyteller. They are the foundation upon which all other aspects of storytelling are built.

Character Development

Characters are the lifeblood of your story. They are the vehicles through which the plot unfolds, and readers connect emotionally with them. A well-developed character is more than just a name on a page; they have desires, fears, strengths, and flaws that make them feel real.

Every character in your book has a story arc.

Even if you are writing a memoir – YOU are the character! If you are writing a Non-Fiction book- YOUR READER is the character! A compelling character arc is a journey that a character goes through in a story. It involves facing fears and overcoming challenges, ultimately leading to personal growth. When you think about your favorite stories and characters from literature and film, you may notice that they all have a well-crafted character arc. Constructing a solid character arc can turn a good character into a great one and improve your writing significantly.

What is a Character Arc? A character arc refers to the journey a character undergoes throughout a story. This journey involves facing adversity and challenges, experiencing changes and growth, and ultimately finding a resolution. The character arc usually follows the Hero's Journey and traditional three-act story structure. For most protagonist character arcs, the journey begins with an inciting incident that sets up the stakes and central conflict for the character. The arc's progress depends on the story type and the character's role. How to

Understanding how character arcs work and the broad categories most arcs fall into is essential to charting your arcs.

Whether you are writing a good character who will undergo a negative character arc or vice versa, there are some tips to consider as you plan out your character's arc and flesh out your character development. Genre often informs the way that your character arcs will unfold. If you are writing a tragedy, your protagonist will most likely undergo a negative arc, ending the story at a much lower point than where it began. If you are writing an inspirational story, you will probably have a character change for the better and follow a positive character arc. Some characters have more elaborate character arcs than others.

A good story generally has a robust set of well-fleshed-out characters in addition to the protagonist. Knowing what role characters play in your story will help inform their character needs and the shape their arc will take. For instance, if your story has a clear-cut protagonist and an antagonist, they will likely have opposite character arcs.

It is essential to have a strong outline with an apparent first, second, and third act before mapping out character arcs. Characters change alongside your larger narrative. Knowing where a critical plot point or turning point might be will help you map out a corresponding character arc.

There are several archetypal character arcs. Most of these arcs are change arcs where we witness a character's transformation throughout the story, either in a positive or negative direction. A less common arc form is the flat arc, where a character remains unchanged throughout the story.

1. **Transformational arc:** A transformational arc is a character arc in which the protagonist undergoes a significant change from an ordinary person to a hero throughout the story. This character development is expected in epic tales and the

classic hero's journey narrative structure. For instance, Harry Potter, the protagonist in the Harry Potter series, starts as an orphaned young boy living with his cruel Aunt and Uncle, who treat him like a servant. As the story progresses, we witness Harry summoning his inner strength and ultimately becoming the savior of the wizarding world.

2. **Positive change arc:** A positive change arc is similar to a transformational arc but not as dramatic. It requires a character to experience positive change throughout the story. At the story's beginning, characters often have negative outlooks or traits that evolve into an optimistic worldview by the end. For example, in "A Christmas Carol," Ebenezer Scrooge begins as a wealthy old miser obsessed with greed. However, as the story progresses, he transforms significantly and becomes benevolent and charitable.

3. **Negative change arc:** A negative change arc refers to a character's transformation from being excellent or virtuous to becoming evil or experiencing misfortune throughout a story. For instance, in "The Godfather," Michael Corleone is initially portrayed as a clean army veteran with a good reputation despite being part of a New York organized crime family. However, by the end of the story, Michael's character arc has descended into negativity, and he has become the head of the crime family, driven by a ruthless desire to maintain control and power. In the TV series "Breaking Bad," Walter White starts as a struggling public school chemistry teacher, desperate to provide for his family. However, as the series progresses, Walter's character arc takes an adverse turn, and he compromises his morals to become a successful drug kingpin, ultimately destroying his family and his happiness.

4. **Flat or static character arc:** A flat arc is a rare character arc commonly seen in action and thriller stories. For instance, Indiana Jones is an emotionally stoic and competent adventurer who maintains his demeanor regardless of the danger he faces. In action-adventure, screenwriting is expected to create flat protagonists who remain calm and relaxed under pressure.

Tools: Character Breakdown Worksheet:

Create fully realized characters using a character breakdown worksheet. Creating a map of your character's Hero's Journey would be best. The following section will show a breakdown of The Here's Journey.

The character breakdown sheet helps you explore your character's background, motivations, and relationships. Consider their childhood, education, family life, and critical experiences that shaped their identity. Ask questions like:

- o   What are their goals and dreams?
- o   What are their biggest fears and weaknesses?

- How do they change throughout the story?
- What relationships are central to their development?

By thoroughly understanding your characters, you can create more authentic and engaging interactions, making it easier for readers to become invested in their journey.

One thing I like to do is interview my characters. It's a fun role-playing exercise you can do alone or with a friend. Ask them questions about themselves. It might surprise you and offer new ideas. Perhaps you learn they don't eat fish and why. That may create an opportunity in the book to help your reader know something about them that moves the story along in exciting ways without expositional (You'll learn more about what this means in the following few chapters.)

Here is an example of a character breakdown worksheet:

Character Breakdown Sheet

1. **Basic Information**
    - **Full Name:**
    - **Nickname(s):**
    - **Age:**
    - **Date of Birth:**
    - **Gender:**
    - **Occupation:**
    - **Nationality/Background:**
    - **Education:**

2. **Physical Appearance**
    - **Height:**
    - **Weight:**
    - **Build (e.g., slender, muscular):**
    - **Hair Color/Style:**
    - **Eye Color:**
    - **Skin Tone:**

- Distinguishing Features (e.g., scars, tattoos):
- Typical Clothing Style:

3. **Personality**
    - Strengths:
    - Weaknesses:
    - Hobbies/Interests:
    - Fears/Phobias:
    - Quirks/Habits:
    - Values/Beliefs:
    - Motivations:
    - Goals (short-term and long-term):
    - Secrets:

4. **Background and History**
    - Family (parents, siblings, etc.):
    - Significant Past Events:
    - Childhood and Upbringing:
    - Meaningful Relationships (friends, mentors, rivals):
    - Past Achievements/Failures:

5. **Relationships**
    - Romantic Interests:
    - Best Friends:
    - Allies:
    - Enemies/Rivals:
    - Mentors:
    - Significant Others:

6. **Role in the Story**
    - Protagonist/Antagonist/Supporting Character:
    - Character Arc (how they change throughout the story):
    - Conflict (internal and external):
    - Key Actions/Decisions:
    - Resolution/Outcome:

7. **Dialogue and Voice**
    - Speech Patterns (formal, informal, accent, etc.):
    - Catchphrases/Unique Expressions:

8. **Miscellaneous**
    - Favorite Things (food, music, etc.):
    - Pet Peeves:
    - Preferred Social Settings:
    - Life Philosophy:

Plot Structure and Pacing

The plot is the backbone of your story. It is the sequence of events that moves the narrative forward. A well-structured plot keeps the reader engaged, balancing moments of tension and resolution.

- **Exposition**: Introduce the setting, characters, and basic premise.
- **Rising Action:** Build tension through conflict and obstacles.
- **Climax**: The turning point where the central conflict reaches its peak.
- **Falling Action:** The consequences of the climax unfold.
- **Resolution**: The story's conclusion, where loose ends are tied up.

Pacing is equally essential. The speed at which your story unfolds can significantly affect its impact. Too slow, and you risk losing your reader's interest; too fast, and you might need to give them more time to connect with the characters or understand the stakes. Vary your pacing by balancing action scenes with quieter moments of reflection or dialogue.

The Hero's Journey and Other Story Structures

I am a big fan of The Hero's Journey. Every great film or story, from ancient myths to modern blockbusters, uses this model whether the writers realize it. Once you've begun exploring and using it as a tool in your writing, you will see it in the books and films you read. The concept was popularized by Joseph Campbell, an American mythologist, writer, and lecturer, in his book "The Hero with a Thousand Faces" (1949).

I will outline other models as well. Find the model that works best for you and your story.

Starting Your Book in the Middle: A Strategic Approach

It's not uncommon for writers to feel the urge to begin their story in the middle of the action or with a compelling hook that grabs the reader's attention right from the first page. This technique, often referred to as in medias res (Latin for "into the middle of things"), can be a powerful way to engage your audience and create immediate intrigue. However, while this approach can be highly effective, it also requires careful planning to ensure that the narrative remains coherent and that essential plot points are preserved.

1. **The Importance of a Linear Outline:** Before diving into a non-linear structure, it's crucial to map your story in a straightforward, chronological timeline. This means outlining your plot from beginning to end, ensuring that all key events, character arcs, and story beats are clearly defined. By doing this, you fully understand how each element of your story fits together and how the narrative flows naturally over time.

2. **Why Start with a Linear Outline?**

    - **Coherence**: A linear outline helps maintain the coherence of your plot. When you understand the natural progression of events, you can more easily manipulate the timeline without losing the logical flow of the story.

    - **Character Development:** Characters often undergo significant growth throughout a story. Outlining linearly ensures that their development remains consistent, even if the narrative is later restructured.

    - **Plot Points and Beats:** Identifying crucial plot points and beats in a linear format helps you avoid accidentally omitting important information or scenes when rearranging the story's order.

3. **Playing with Narrative Structure:** Once you have a solid linear outline, you can experiment with the order of events. Here are a few strategies you might consider:

    - **Starting with a Climactic Moment:** Beginning your story at a high point or with a significant event can hook readers immediately. For instance, beginning with a scene from the middle of the story can create suspense and curiosity, making readers eager to find out how the characters arrived at that moment.

- **Flashbacks and Flashforwards:** After establishing an exciting opening, you can weave in flashbacks or flashforwards to fill in the backstory or hint at future events. This technique can add depth and complexity to your narrative, enriching the reader's experience.

- **Dual Timelines:** Some stories benefit from parallel narratives that unfold in different periods but are interconnected. Switching between timelines can build tension and draw parallels between past and present or different character perspectives.

4. **Maintaining Narrative Integrity:** As you rearrange the pieces of your story, it's essential to constantly refer back to your original linear outline. This ensures that, despite the shifts in chronology, the story remains clear and that the progression of events still makes sense. Consider how each scene's placement affects the reader's understanding and emotional engagement with the story.

5. **Balancing Creativity with Structure:** The beauty of storytelling lies in its flexibility; you can play with time, perspective, and sequence to craft a unique narrative experience. However, this creativity should always be balanced with structure. Grounding your story in a well-thought-out linear outline allows you to explore non-linear storytelling without sacrificing clarity or coherence.

Tools: The Hero's Journey Map and Worksheet

1. **The Ordinary World**

    - **Describe the hero's everyday life before the adventure begins:**
        - What is the hero's environment like?
        - What are their everyday challenges?
        - How does the hero fit into their world?

2. **The Call to Adventure**

    - **What event or situation triggers the hero's journey?**
        - What prompts the hero to leave their ordinary world?
        - Is this call internal (a feeling or realization) or external (an event or encounter)?

3. **Refusal of the Call**

    - **How does the hero initially react to the call to adventure?**
        - What fears or doubts do they have?
        - What are the consequences of refusing the call?

4. **Meeting the Mentor**

    - **Who is the mentor that guides the hero?**
        - What knowledge or tools does the mentor provide?
        - How does the mentor influence the hero's decision to embark on the journey?

5. **Crossing the Threshold**

    - **Describe the moment the hero fully commits to the journey:**
        - What obstacles must the hero overcome to start their adventure?
        - How does the hero feel as they leave the Ordinary World behind?

6. **Tests, Allies, and Enemies**

    - **List the challenges the hero faces and the allies/enemies they encounter:**
        - What tests help the hero grow stronger or more knowledgeable?
        - Who are the hero's allies, and how do they support the journey?
        - Who are the enemies or antagonists that create conflict?

7. **Approach to the Inmost Cave**
    - **What is the hero's greatest challenge or ordeal leading up to the climax?**
        - How does the hero prepare for this challenge?
        - What fears or uncertainties must the hero confront?

8. **The Ordeal**
    - **Describe the hero's most difficult test or moment of crisis:**
        - What is at stake during this ordeal?
        - How does the hero face this challenge, and what do they learn from it?

9. **The Reward (Seizing the Sword)**
    - **What does the hero gain after overcoming the ordeal?**
        - Is it a tangible reward, like a treasure, or an intangible one, like wisdom or strength?
        - How does this reward change the hero?

10. **The Road Back**
    - **What challenges does the hero face on the journey home?**
        - How does the hero's return journey differ from their initial departure?
        - Are there any unresolved conflicts or final tests?

11. **The Resurrection**
    - **Describe the hero's final, transformative ordeal:**
        - What ultimate test does the hero face?
        - How does the hero emerge changed, and how does this transformation impact the story's resolution?

12. **Return with the Elixir**
    - **How does the hero return to the Ordinary World?**
        - What "elixir" (knowledge, power, love, etc.) does the hero bring back?
        - How does the hero's return affect the world or people they left behind?
    - **Character Development:** Outline each of your character's Hero's Journey. Jot down any additional notes about the hero's growth and relationships with other characters.

- **Theme**: Reflect on the central themes or messages that are reinforced by the hero's journey.
- **Plot Twists:** Consider any unexpected turns or surprises that may arise during the journey.

A classic example of a book that uses the Hero's Journey as its guide is "The Hobbit" by J.R.R. Tolkien.

Hero's Journey in "The Hobbit"

1. **Ordinary World:**

    o   Bilbo Baggins lives a comfortable, unremarkable life in his hobbit hole in the Shire. He values peace, quiet, and predictability.

2. **Call to Adventure:**

    o   The wizard Gandalf arrives, inviting Bilbo to join a group of dwarves on a quest to reclaim their homeland and treasure from the dragon Smaug. Bilbo initially refuses, preferring his quiet life.

3. **Refusal of the Call:**

    o   Bilbo is hesitant and resistant, not wanting to leave his comfortable existence. He doubts his suitability for adventure and feels anxious about the dangers ahead.

4. **Meeting the Mentor:**

    o   Gandalf encourages Bilbo, seeing potential in him that Bilbo does not see in himself. Gandalf gives him advice, provides guidance, and ultimately convinces him to join the dwarves.

5. **Crossing the Threshold:**

    o   Bilbo takes a leap of faith, leaves the Shire, and embarks on the journey with the dwarves, leaving his familiar world behind.

6. **Tests, Allies, and Enemies:**

    o   Throughout the journey, Bilbo faces various challenges and makes new allies, including elves and men. He also encounters enemies, such as trolls, goblins, and giant spiders. He grows in courage and resourcefulness, discovering his talents and capabilities.

7. **Approach to the Inmost Cave:**

    o Bilbo and the dwarves arrive at the Lonely Mountain, where Smaug, the dragon, guards the treasure. This is the most dangerous part of their journey, requiring careful planning and great bravery.

8. **Ordeal:**

    o Bilbo confronts Smaug, using his wit to outsmart the dragon and discover its weakness. This encounter is the story's darkest moment, filled with tension and risk.

9. **Reward (Seizing the Sword):**

    o Bilbo gains possession of a part of the treasure (the Arkenstone) and the courage and confidence to stand up for what he believes is right, even against the wishes of the dwarves.

10. **The Road Back:**

    o After Smaug is killed, the journey is not over. The adventurers face new challenges, including disputes over the treasure and the impending Battle of the Five Armies. Bilbo realizes that his adventure is far from finished.

11. **Resurrection:**

    o In the climactic Battle of the Five Armies, Bilbo's courage and choices are tested once more. He witnesses the cost of greed and conflict but also the value of friendship, honor, and peace.

12. **Return with the Elixir:**

    o Bilbo returns to the Shire, profoundly changed by his experiences. He brings back not only a small share of treasure but also wisdom, courage, and a new perspective on life. He has grown beyond his former self, embodying the transformation of the Hero's Journey.

"Wild" is a powerful example of how the Hero's Journey can be applied to a real-life narrative. It showcases a personal transformation through a journey of physical and emotional challenges, leading to profound growth and change.

Hero's Journey in "Wild"

1. **Ordinary World:**

    o   Cheryl Strayed's life is in turmoil. After the death of her mother, her family falls apart, and she spirals into self-destructive behavior, including drug use and a failed marriage. She feels lost and disconnected from her true self.

2. **Call to Adventure:**

    o   In the midst of her grief and confusion, Cheryl decides to hike the Pacific Crest Trail (PCT), a 1,100-mile journey from the Mojave Desert to the Oregon-Washington border. The call comes from within—a desire to find herself and heal from her past trauma.

3. **Refusal of the Call:**

    o   Cheryl has doubts about her ability to complete the hike. She is inexperienced, unprepared, and unsure if this journey will bring her the solace she is seeking.

4. **Meeting the Mentor:**

    o   Although there isn't a single mentor, Cheryl meets various people along the way who provide guidance, support, and advice, including other hikers, park rangers, and even strangers who help her. The trail itself becomes a mentor, teaching her resilience, patience, and self-reliance.

5. **Crossing the Threshold:**

    o   Cheryl commits to the journey by stepping onto the trail, leaving her old life and familiar world behind. She faces immediate challenges, such as carrying an overly heavy backpack and navigating difficult terrain, but she perseveres.

6. **Tests, Allies, and Enemies:**

    o   As she progresses, Cheryl encounters both physical and emotional challenges: harsh weather, exhaustion, injury, hunger, and fear. She also meets other hikers who become allies, sharing experiences and camaraderie, and faces moments of danger that test her resolve.

7. **Approach to the Inmost Cave:**

    o   Cheryl reaches the most difficult and remote parts of the trail, where she must confront her deepest fears and pain. She faces moments of profound loneliness and doubt, questioning her reasons for being on the trail and whether she will make it to the end.

8. **Ordeal:**
   - The ordeal comes in moments of crisis where Cheryl confronts the emotional weight of her mother's death, her past mistakes, and her feelings of guilt and regret. She battles through both physical hardships and the inner demons that have haunted her.

9. **Reward (Seizing the Sword):**
   - Cheryl experiences moments of clarity, healing, and self-realization. She discovers her inner strength, resilience, and capacity for self-love. She gains a deeper understanding of herself and her past, finding peace with her mother's death and forgiveness for her own mistakes.

10. **The Road Back:**
    - Cheryl continues her journey, but now with a renewed sense of purpose and clarity. She faces additional challenges, but they no longer deter her. She becomes more focused on completing her journey and returning home with her newfound wisdom.

11. **Resurrection:**
    - As she nears the end of the PCT, Cheryl emerges transformed—stronger, more self-aware, and ready to face the world with a new perspective. She has survived the ordeal and gained a profound understanding of herself and life.

12. **Return with the Elixir:**
    - Cheryl completes the trail, having found a sense of healing, redemption, and inner peace. She returns to her ordinary world with the "elixir" of self-discovery, ready to build a new life and share her story, which later becomes the basis for her memoir "Wild."

"The Power of Habit" by Charles Duhigg uses the Hero's Journey framework to guide readers through the process of understanding and transforming habits. It positions readers as the heroes of their own stories, capable of achieving meaningful change through knowledge, perseverance, and action.

Hero's Journey in "The Power of Habit"

1. **Ordinary World:**

    o   The book begins by exploring the ordinary world of habits—behaviors that people perform automatically, often without realizing their impact on personal and professional lives. It introduces the science of habits and explains how they govern much of our daily routines.

2. **Call to Adventure:**

    o   The call to adventure comes with the realization that understanding and changing habits can significantly improve various areas of life, from health to productivity. This call challenges readers to examine their habits and consider the potential for personal transformation.

3. **Refusal of the Call:**

    o   The refusal is the skepticism or resistance readers might feel when confronted with the idea that they can change deeply ingrained behaviors. Many believe their habits are too fixed or that change is too difficult to achieve.

4. **Meeting the Mentor:**

    o   Duhigg becomes a mentor figure, providing readers with knowledge, research, and tools to understand the "habit loop" (cue, routine, reward) and how it operates. He offers stories of real-life individuals and organizations who successfully changed habits, showing what is possible.

5. **Crossing the Threshold:**

    o   Readers cross the threshold by applying the book's principles to their lives. This may involve identifying a specific habit they wish to change, understanding its components, and beginning the process of experimenting with new routines.

6. **Tests, Allies, and Enemies:**

    o   As readers begin to change their habits, they face tests (such as resisting temptations and maintaining motivation), allies (support from others who encourage and assist in habit change), and enemies (internal resistance, societal pressures, or environments that reinforce old habits).

7. **Approach to the Inmost Cave:**

    o   The approach involves deeper challenges and setbacks as readers attempt to reshape more difficult habits or face relapses. Duhigg provides strategies to overcome these obstacles, such as using "keystone habits" that trigger positive changes in other areas of life.

8. **Ordeal:**

   o   The ordeal is the struggle to sustain new habits and resist the powerful pull of old behaviors. Readers confront the core of their motivations, beliefs, and the obstacles preventing them from achieving their desired change.

9. **Reward (Seizing the Sword):**

   o   The reward is the realization that habits can be changed and that the effort to do so leads to positive outcomes. Readers experience the benefits of new habits, such as improved health, productivity, and well-being.

10. **The Road Back:**

    o   Having achieved some success, readers face the challenge of maintaining their new habits over time, adapting to new circumstances, and reinforcing the changes they have made.

11. **Resurrection:**

    o   The resurrection involves a renewed commitment to habit change, often after experiencing setbacks or challenges. Readers emerge with a deeper understanding of how habits work and a stronger ability to shape their behaviors.

12. **Return with the Elixir:**

    o   Readers return to their ordinary world with the "elixir"—a powerful understanding of the science of habits and the tools to transform them. They are equipped to apply these insights to various aspects of life, achieving long-term change and growth.

Case Studies for the different types of story structures – Three Act Structure, Freytag's Pyramid, The Seven Point Structure

- **Three-Act Structure:** Divides the story into three parts: Setup, Confrontation, and Resolution.

- **Freytag's Pyramid:** A five-part structure that includes Exposition, Rising Action, Climax, Falling Action, and Denouement.

- **The Seven-Point Structure:** Focuses on key plot points, including the Hook, Plot Turn 1, Pinch Point 1, Midpoint, Pinch Point 2, Plot Turn 2, and Resolution.

Each structure offers a different approach to pacing and tension, and the choice of structure should align with the goals of your story.

Three-Act Structure

Aristotle said that the perfect story structure is a three-act affair. The basic three-act structure divides a narrative into three parts: setup, confrontation, and resolution. It's an easy way to structure your life story. The setup introduces the characters, their relationships, and their environment. Additionally, it presents a strong hook, which is an exciting incident that provokes a change in the protagonist's routine. The second act, the confrontation, is the central part of the story. The stakes are raised throughout the act until a major twist. Usually, a moment of crisis initiates the start of act three, the resolution. The resolution presents the final showdown and, draws together, and explains all the different strands of the plot. If your timeline can be divided into three clear sections along the lines of these themes, then this could be the structure for you. A "Three Act" book is often written chronologically, but it doesn't have to be.

A great example of the Basic Three Act structure is "Pride and Prejudice" by Jane Austen.

The setup introduces Elizabeth Bennet, who clashes with the wealthy and seemingly arrogant Mr. Darcy.

The confrontation occurs when Darcy unexpectedly proposes to Elizabeth, who rejects him due to her prejudice and misunderstandings. Darcy responds with a letter explaining his actions, prompting Elizabeth to reconsider her initial judgments.

The resolution unfolds as Darcy redeems himself by helping Elizabeth's family in a crisis. This leads to a second, sincere proposal, which Elizabeth accepts. The story concludes with their marriage and newfound understanding, overcoming their initial pride and prejudice.

Act One: The Setup Some people refer to the moment when the story is set in motion as the 'inciting incident.'

Act Two: The Conflict: This is where your characters start going through significant changes (the pros call it character arc) as a result of what's happening.

Act Three: The Climax The resolution is where our characters face the central problem, the story starts to make sense, and we tie up any loose ends (also known as the 'denouement'). According to Aristotle, it's important that all the events in the story are interconnected and that the plot elicits an emotional response from the audience. We agree with Aristotle on this point.

Another great book that uses the three-act structure is "The Great Gatsby" by F. Scott Fitzgerald.

The Writer's Room

Three-Act Structure in "The Great Gatsby"

Act 1: The Setup

- The story begins with Nick Carraway, the narrator, moving to West Egg, Long Island, where he becomes intrigued by his mysterious neighbor, Jay Gatsby, a wealthy man known for his lavish parties.

- We are introduced to Daisy Buchanan, Nick's cousin, and her husband, Tom, who live in East Egg. Gatsby is revealed to be deeply in love with Daisy, whom he met years ago before she married Tom. The inciting incident occurs when Gatsby requests Nick to arrange a meeting between him and Daisy, reigniting their old romance.

Act 2: The Conflict

- Tension builds as Gatsby and Daisy rekindle their relationship, and Tom becomes suspicious. Gatsby's desire to recreate the past and win Daisy over fully intensifies the conflict. A climactic confrontation occurs when Tom, Gatsby, Daisy, Nick, and Jordan Baker confront their tangled emotions in a New York City hotel. Tom exposes Gatsby's questionable past and illegal activities, attempting to undermine Gatsby in Daisy's eyes.

Act 3: The Climax

- The climax occurs when Daisy, driving Gatsby's car, accidentally kills Tom's mistress, Myrtle Wilson. Gatsby decides to take the blame to protect Daisy. The resolution follows with Gatsby's tragic death, shot by Myrtle's husband, who believes Gatsby was driving the car. The story concludes with Nick reflecting on the events, disillusioned by the moral decay and the unattainable nature of the American Dream.

"The Great Gatsby" uses the three-act structure to effectively build suspense, develop complex characters, and convey its themes of love, wealth, and the American Dream.

Structure of Freytag's Pyramid

Freytag's Pyramid breaks down a story into five main parts, representing the rise and fall of the narrative's action:

1. **Exposition**
    - This is the story's introduction, where the setting, characters, and basic situation are established. The exposition sets the stage for the events that follow and provides the audience with the necessary background information.

2. **Rising Action**
    - After the exposition, the story builds tension through a series of events and conflicts. These complications lead to the central conflict. The rising action is crucial as it develops the plot and deepens the characters, driving the narrative toward the climax.

3. **Climax**
    - The climax is the turning point or the most intense moment of the story. It's where the central conflict reaches its peak. The outcome of the climax will set the direction for the rest of the story. It's often the moment of greatest suspense or emotion.

4. **Falling Action**
    - Following the climax, the falling action involves the events that result from the climax. It is where the tension begins to decrease, and the story starts moving towards its conclusion. Conflicts start to resolve, and the consequences of the climax are explored.

5. **Denouement (or Resolution)**
    - The denouement is the final part of the story, where all the loose ends are tied up, the conflicts are resolved, and the story concludes. It provides closure to the narrative, giving the audience a sense of completion.

Importance of Freytag's Pyramid

Freytag's Pyramid is an essential tool for writers and literary analysts because it provides a clear framework for understanding the structure of a narrative. It helps to break down a story's components to see how they interact and contribute to the overall plot. This model is beneficial for classical dramas but can be adapted to analyze novels, short stories, and other narrative forms.

The Pyramid emphasizes the importance of rising action and climax in creating a compelling story, as these are the points where the reader or audience is most engaged. Understanding this structure allows writers to craft stories that maintain interest and build towards a satisfying conclusion.

Here's a classic story that uses Freytag's Pyramid:

"Romeo and Juliet" by William Shakespeare. Although this is a play, it is often studied as a literary work that follows Freytag's five-act structure, which is foundational to Freytag's Pyramid.

Freytag's Pyramid in "Romeo and Juliet"

1. **Exposition:**

    o   The story begins in Verona, where the longstanding feud between the Montagues and Capulets is introduced. We meet the main characters, including Romeo Montague and Juliet Capulet, who are from the two feuding families. Their respective situations are established, as is the tension that drives the plot.

2. **Rising Action:**

    o   Romeo and Juliet meet at a Capulet party and instantly fall in love despite knowing they are from enemy families. They secretly marry the next day, setting off a series of escalating conflicts. The rising action includes Tybalt challenging Romeo to a duel, Mercutio's death, and Romeo killing Tybalt in revenge, leading to his banishment.

3. **Climax:**

    o   The climax occurs when Juliet is informed of her arranged marriage to Paris, and Romeo is banished. The tension reaches its peak when Juliet takes a potion to fake her death, hoping to be reunited with Romeo, but the plan goes awry.

4. **Falling Action:**

    o   The falling action follows Romeo's discovery of Juliet's apparent death. Devastated, he returns to Verona, buys poison, and visits Juliet's tomb. Meanwhile, Juliet awakens to find Romeo dead beside her.

5. **Denouement (Resolution):**

    o   In the denouement, Juliet takes her own life with Romeo's dagger upon discovering his death. The deaths of the young lovers ultimately lead to a reconciliation between the Montagues and Capulets as they realize the tragic consequences of their feud.

"Romeo and Juliet" is a classic example of Freytag's Pyramid, which uses a clear structure of exposition, rising action, climax, falling action, and resolution to build and release tension, culminating in a tragic ending that serves as a moral lesson on the destructive power of hatred and conflict.

The Seven-Point Structure

The Seven-Point Structure is a plot framework designed to help writers outline their stories by focusing on seven key plot points that guide the narrative from beginning to end. This structure is particularly popular among fantasy and science fiction writers but can be adapted to any genre. The framework helps ensure the story remains well-paced and cohesive, building toward a satisfying conclusion.

The Seven Points

1. **The Hook**

    o **What is it?** The hook is the starting point of your story. It's the event or situation that grabs the reader's attention and introduces the protagonist in their everyday world.

    o **Purpose**: To establish the protagonist's status quo and to pique the reader's curiosity.

2. **Plot Turn 1**

    o What is it? This is the event that changes everything for the protagonist and sets the main story in motion. It's where the protagonist's ordinary world is disrupted, often by an external conflict or problem that needs to be resolved.

    o Purpose: To propel the protagonist into the central conflict of the story.

3. **Pinch Point 1**

    o What is it? The first pinch point is a reminder of the central conflict or the antagonist's power. It's a moment of tension that puts pressure on the protagonist and raises the stakes.

    o Purpose: To reinforce the threat or challenge the protagonist is facing, keeping the tension high.

4. **The Midpoint**

    o What is it? The midpoint is the pivotal moment where the protagonist makes a significant decision or action that changes the direction of the story. It often involves a revelation or a shift in the protagonist's understanding of their situation.

    o Purpose: To deepen the plot and increase the protagonist's commitment to the story's outcome.

5. **Pinch Point 2**

    o What is it? The second pinch point further escalates the tension, often by showing the antagonist's strength or by putting the protagonist in a seemingly hopeless situation.

    o Purpose: To push the protagonist toward the climax, forcing them to confront their biggest challenge.

6. **Plot Turn 2**

    o What is it? This is the event that leads directly to the climax. It's often a moment of revelation or a final piece of the puzzle that empowers the protagonist to face the antagonist or resolve the central conflict.

o Purpose: To transition the story from the buildup to the climax, setting the stage for the final confrontation.

7. **The Resolution**

    o What is it? The resolution is the conclusion of the story, where the central conflict is resolved, and the protagonist's journey comes to an end. It provides closure and often reflects on how the protagonist has changed as a result of their experiences.

    o Purpose: To tie up loose ends and leave the reader with a sense of satisfaction.

Why Use the Seven-Point Structure?

The Seven-Point Structure is useful because it provides a clear, flexible framework for constructing a well-paced and engaging story. It helps writers to focus on the essential moments in the narrative, ensuring that each part of the story builds logically and effectively toward the climax and resolution.

This structure is particularly helpful in genres that involve complex plots, as it allows for careful planning and ensures that crucial plot points are aligned with the story's overall arc. By using the Seven-Point Structure, writers can create dynamic and emotionally resonant stories, keeping readers engaged from beginning to end.

A great example of a book that follows the seven-point story structure is "Harry Potter and the Philosopher's Stone" (also known as "Harry Potter and the Sorcerer's Stone") by J.K. Rowling. This book exemplifies how to use the seven-point structure to build a compelling and satisfying narrative arc.

Here's how "Harry Potter and the Philosopher's Stone" aligns with the seven-point structure:

1. The Hook

The story begins with a hook that establishes Harry's ordinary world. We meet Harry Potter, an orphaned boy living with his abusive aunt, uncle, and cousin. He's treated poorly and lives a dull, unhappy life under the stairs, unaware of his true heritage. This sets the stage for the journey to come and establishes the protagonist's status quo, which will soon be disrupted.

2. Plot Turn 1 (Inciting Incident)

Harry receives a letter from Hogwarts, and Hagrid comes to inform him that he is a wizard. This is the moment when Harry is introduced to the wizarding world, which changes his life forever. It sets him on a new path away from his old life and into the adventure of discovering his true identity.

3. Pinch Point 1

Harry arrives at Hogwarts and begins to experience the challenges of this new world, including learning about magic, meeting friends like Hermione and Ron, and encountering antagonists like Draco Malfoy and Professor Snape. This pinch point emphasizes the dangers and stakes in the wizarding world, including hints of Voldemort's influence and Harry's connection to him.

4. Midpoint (The Twist)

The midpoint comes when Harry, Ron, and Hermione discover the mystery of the Philosopher's Stone and the possible threat it poses in the wrong hands. They realize that someone is trying to steal the stone and that Voldemort may be involved. This revelation raises the stakes and makes the conflict more urgent, shifting the story from a learning phase to a mission to protect the stone.

5. Pinch Point 2

The second pinch point occurs when the trio faces obstacles that intensify the conflict. They learn about the protections around the stone and must get past Fluffy, the three-headed dog, and other magical traps. Harry also has a direct encounter with Voldemort (through Quirrell), making the threat real and immediate. This moment reinforces the antagonist's power and the hero's vulnerability.

6. Plot Turn 2 (Climax)

The climax is reached when Harry confronts Professor Quirrell, who is possessed by Voldemort, in the final chamber. Harry has to face his greatest fear and the darkest force in the wizarding world. This is the ultimate test of his courage, strength, and identity. The outcome of this confrontation will determine the fate of the stone and his own future.

7. Resolution

After the battle, Harry awakens in the hospital wing, learning that he has defeated Voldemort (at least temporarily) and protected the Philosopher's Stone. The resolution ties up loose ends: Harry gains a sense of belonging in the wizarding world, establishes his friendships, and returns to the Dursleys for the summer, but now with the knowledge that he is not alone and is valued.

Setting and World-Building (for Fiction)

For fiction writers, particularly those working in genres like fantasy, science fiction, or historical fiction, world-building is a critical part of the storytelling process. The setting is more than just a backdrop; it's a living, breathing world that influences the characters and plot.

- World-building involves creating a detailed environment where your story takes place. This includes the physical landscape and the social, political, and cultural dynamics that shape the world. Consider questions like:
    o What is the history of this world?
    o What are the societal norms and laws?
    o What technology, magic, or belief systems exist?
    o How does the setting influence the characters' lives and decisions?

A richly developed world adds depth and realism to your story, making it easier for readers to immerse themselves in the narrative.

Ok- that was a lot of technical information about story structure. Important but a little heady, I know.

I've always believed that you're better at breaking the rules once you know them. While each of those story structure outlines are tried and true, again, play with them within the context of your story/book.

When writing, I engage all the tools in my toolbox, reaching into every aspect of my being. So, we just had a conversation with the brain about the "rules." Now, let's talk about connecting to your cosmic co-writer.

Dreamwork for Storytelling

Using Dreamwork for world building and storytelling:

It may seem weird that I am talking about dreamwork in a book about writing; however, dreamwork is an incredible tool for generating fresh ideas, particularly when crafting new worlds for your creative projects. It's also where my friend BoB and I have the most fun together.

Dreams have the uncanny ability to tap into the subconscious, revealing new perspectives, unique concepts, and surprising details that can bring a special magic to your work—whether you're writing a novel, a nonfiction work, making a film, or working on any other creative pursuit.

Keep a notebook, pen, or a dream app by your bed to start using dreamwork in your creative process. As you begin to fall asleep, ask your subconscious a specific question. For instance, you might whisper to yourself, "Take me to the fairylands tonight and help me learn their language," or "What does a wood fairy eat?" By framing such vivid and specific prompts, you're inviting your mind to explore creative possibilities while you sleep.

If you don't have a specific question in mind, consider using a more open-ended prompt, like "What does my story need that I'm missing?" This kind of approach allows your mind to wander freely, uncovering new ideas or elements that could add depth to your project.

When you wake up, take a few moments to jot down any dreams, images, or impressions that come to mind. These fragments often hold the seeds of inspiration, pointing you toward new directions, details, or solutions that you might not have consciously considered. Think of your dreams as a bridge to deeper creativity, and make it a habit to capture them before they fade away.

By regularly practicing dreamwork, you will find that your creative projects become richer with unexpected insights, vivid details, and fresh perspectives, all drawn from the vast landscape of your subconscious mind.

But dreamwork is more than just a nocturnal activity. As you start engaging with your dreams, you'll begin to open a space that allows you to connect with your cosmic writing co-pilot, even in your waking hours. For me, that co-pilot is BoB. Sometimes, when I feel particularly stuck, I pause and ask BoB for guidance—to help me solve a problem, spark an idea, or reveal what the story needs next.

Practicing this kind of connection with your guides strengthens your intuitive abilities, making it easier to access all those "hidden" ideas that are quietly percolating in the depths of your mind. It creates a sense of partnership between your conscious and subconscious selves, and it's a powerful way to keep your creativity flowing, even when you're not actively working on your project.

Deepening Your Connection with Your Dream World

The more you engage with your dreams, the clearer the communication becomes. It's like learning a new language; the more you practice, the more fluent you become. Your subconscious begins to trust that you're listening. In response, it offers up more vivid, detailed dreams filled with symbols and scenarios that can provide rich material for your creative endeavors.

You might find yourself dreaming of places you've never been or experiencing emotions that don't quite fit into your waking life. Don't dismiss these as mere oddities; instead, treat them as gifts from your mind, providing a new lens through which to view your project. A fleeting image from a dream might inspire the setting for a story, while an unresolved feeling could become the emotional core of a character.

Over time, you may start to notice patterns or recurring symbols in your dreams. Pay attention to these—they are the language of your subconscious. For instance, if you keep dreaming of doors, think about what they might symbolize for you. Are they gateways to new opportunities or barriers that need to be overcome? By interpreting these symbols, you can gain deeper insights into your creative work and your own psyche.

Techniques for Remembering and Working with Dreams

To get the most out of your dream work, it's helpful to develop some strategies for remembering your dreams. Start by making it a habit to write down whatever you remember as soon as you wake up, even if it's just a fragment or a feeling. The more you practice this, the better you'll become at recalling your dreams in detail.

Another effective technique is to repeat a mantra to yourself before you fall asleep, such as, "I will remember my dreams." This simple affirmation can prime your mind to be more aware of your dreams and retain them upon waking.

You might also consider creating a "dream altar" near your bed—an area where you place objects that remind you of your creative goals. These could be things like a feather, a small piece of artwork, or a photograph. This physical space serves as a daily reminder to honor your dreams and pay attention to the messages they offer.

Inviting Your Subconscious to Play

One of the most powerful aspects of dreamwork is its ability to make creativity feel like play rather than work. When you invite your subconscious mind to contribute ideas, you're not just brainstorming; you're engaging in a kind of imaginative play that can yield truly unexpected results.

You might discover that some of your best ideas come when you're not trying to force them. For example, I was writing a script about a woman who keeps having the same dream. Ironic, I know. I asked BoB to show me what my character's dream looked like so that I could fully set the scene visually. That night, I dreamed of a barren landscape slowly blooming into a garden, and I woke up knowing exactly how to write the scene.

Embracing the Unknown

Dreamwork also teaches you to embrace the unknown. It encourages you to trust that not everything needs to be planned out in advance. Sometimes, the best ideas come when you surrender control and let your subconscious mind take the lead. Dreams are inherently mysterious, often defying logic and reason, but that's precisely what makes them so valuable for creative work. They encourage you to think outside the box, to explore the unexpected, and to find beauty in ambiguity.

Learning to work with your dreams also means learning to be comfortable with uncertainty. Not every dream will make sense right away, and that's okay. The important thing is to keep an open mind and stay curious. Over time, you'll learn to recognize which dreams are offering creative clues and which ones are just processing the day's events.

Making Dreamwork a Daily Habit

Incorporating dreamwork into your daily routine doesn't have to be time-consuming. Even just a few minutes each morning spent jotting down dream fragments can make a huge difference. The key is consistency. The more you make dreamwork a habit, the more your subconscious mind will respond, offering richer, more detailed dreams for you to explore.

You might find it helpful to set a regular time each day to review your dream notes and see what connections or patterns emerge. Maybe you'll discover that a dream you had last week suddenly seems relevant to a new idea you're working on today. This process of reflection can help you build a deeper relationship with your subconscious and make your creative work more intuitive and inspired.

Trusting Your Inner Guide

Finally, trust in your inner guide—whether that's your subconscious, your creative intuition, or your personal muse like BoB. Trust that you have all the tools you need to bring your creative visions to life. When you hit a creative block, instead of getting frustrated, see it as an opportunity to connect more deeply with your inner world.

Ask yourself, "What would my guide suggest?" or "What if I dream about a solution tonight?" By developing this relationship with your inner guide, you create a powerful ally in your creative journey, one that can help you navigate obstacles, find inspiration in unexpected places, and stay motivated even when the path forward isn't clear.

Here's something I heard George R. Martin share about how he began writing A Song of Fire and Ice

In 1991, while working on another book titled "Avalon," Martin suddenly envisioned a vivid scene that would become the genesis of his epic fantasy series. The scene involved a young boy, who would later be known as Bran Stark, witnessing an execution. In his recollection, Martin frequently emphasizes a specific detail: the discovery of direwolf pups in the "summer snows." He makes a point of highlighting that it was "summer snows," underlining the importance of this imagery in capturing the unique and evocative setting of his story.

To me, this is a perfect example of having a deep connection to his cosmic co-writer and being open to, listening to, and taking note of what might seem like random thoughts and ideas. When we take time to sit with them, contemplate them, and ream on them, who knows what you might end up writing!

Creating a Beat Sheet and Chapter Outline

A Beat Sheet is a tool writers use to outline their story's major beats—or key moments. It's typically used for screenplays, but I also used it for books. It's a step-by-step guide that helps ensure your plot stays on track and that each scene serves a purpose in the overall narrative.

- **Beat Sheet:** Break down your story into individual beats, such as the inciting incident, key turning points, and the climax. Each beat should move the story forward and deepen the reader's understanding of the characters and themes.

- **"And then this happened…":** Use this simple phrase as a guide when outlining each chapter. It helps you focus on cause and effect, ensuring that each event logically leads to the next, creating a cohesive and compelling narrative.

Once you have your beat sheet, you can create a Chapter Outline detailing what happens in each chapter. This outline acts as a roadmap for your writing process, helping you maintain pacing and ensuring that each chapter builds on the one before it. Each chapter should evolve into three parts: a beginning, a middle, and an end. Chapters don't always have to follow the linear plot of your story; this is where you can play with intercutting between characters and storylines.

Chapter lengths can vary widely depending on your genre and the specific demands of your story or subject matter. In fiction, particularly in genres like action, thriller, or mystery, chapters often align with the ebb and flow of the narrative. For instance, an intense action sequence might warrant a shorter, punchier chapter to keep the reader on edge, while a chapter focused on character development or a major plot revelation could be longer to allow for a deeper exploration. A good example of this can be found in Dan Brown's The Da Vinci Code, where short chapters build suspense while longer chapters delve into complex theories or character backstories.

Pacing is crucial here. If your story shifts too quickly between different plots or scenes, you risk confusing or frustrating your reader. Conversely, if you linger too long on a subplot or detail, especially in a genre like action or thriller, you may lose the sense of urgency that keeps your audience engaged. For example, in a romance novel like Pride and Prejudice by Jane Austen, the pacing is more measured, with chapters often dwelling on the subtleties of relationships and societal expectations. Fantasy novels like The Lord of the Rings by J.R.R. Tolkien might have longer chapters to accommodate world-building and intricate plotlines.

In nonfiction, the approach to chapter length can differ significantly. Nonfiction books typically range between 60,000 to 90,000 words, though this is not a strict rule. The key is clarity and conciseness in conveying your ideas. For example, in Malcolm Gladwell's Outliers, chapters vary in length depending on the depth required to explain complex concepts like "The 10,000-Hour Rule" or the cultural legacies that shape success. While word count offers a rough guideline, the quality of your content—how effectively you communicate your message—is far more important than sticking to a specific number of words or pages.

Regardless of your genre or book type, it's essential to keep your reader in mind. Think about the experience you want to create for them. Are you building suspense, providing a deep dive into a topic, or guiding them through a series of thought-provoking ideas? Your chapter lengths, pacing, and structure should all work together to serve that purpose.

Here's an example of a chapter outline: (See if you can spot The Hero's Journey)

Book Title: Ant and the Spider: A Tale of Unexpected Friendship

Chapter 1: The Lost Ant

1.1 A Happy Beginning

- o   Introduction to the ant and its mother
- o   The close bond between the ant and its mother in the bustling anthill
- o   A glimpse of their daily life and the lessons the mother imparts

1.2 The Unexpected Storm

- o   A sudden storm separates the ant from its mother
- o   The ant finds itself lost, scared, and alone in the vast, unfamiliar world
- o   The ant searches desperately for its mother, but the storm makes it impossible

Chapter 2: Alone in the Forest

2.1 The Search Continues

- o   The ant wanders through the forest, encountering various challenges
- o   Meeting different forest creatures, some friendly, others not

2.2 Nightfall and Fear

- o   The ant faces the terrors of night alone, scared of the dark and unfamiliar sounds
- o   Hiding in a small nook, the ant reflects on the warmth and safety of home

2.3 A Silken Shelter

- The ant finds a strange but soft shelter made of silk (a spider's web)
- Exhausted, the ant falls asleep without realizing where it is

Chapter 3: The Spider's Web

3.1 Morning Surprise

- The ant wakes up to find itself in a spider's web, panicking
- The spider, a large but gentle creature, introduces itself and reassures the ant

3.2 The Spider's Kindness

- The spider listens to the ant's story of losing its mother
- Instead of eating the ant, the spider offers to help find the ant's home

3.3 A New Perspective

- The ant's initial fear turns into curiosity about the spider
- The spider shares its own story of loneliness and the desire for a family

Chapter 4: The Journey Together

4.1 Learning to Trust

- The ant hesitates but eventually agrees to let the spider help
- Together, they set out to search for the ant's home, facing challenges along the way

4.2 Overcoming Fears

- The ant gradually overcomes its fear of the spider and other creatures they meet
- The spider protects the ant from dangers, showing a side of spiders the ant never knew

4.3 Building Friendship

- As they travel, the ant and spider bond over their shared experiences
- They learn from each other's strengths and develop a deep, trusting friendship

Chapter 5: Home at Last?

5.1 Nearing the Anthill

- The ant and spider finally find the path leading back to the ant's anthill
- The ant is excited but also conflicted about leaving the spider behind

5.2 A Difficult Decision

- The ant reaches the anthill and sees its fellow ants, but something feels different
- The ant realizes it has grown and changed, no longer fitting in as it once did

5.3 A Heartfelt Goodbye?

- The ant bids farewell to the spider, thanking it for its help
- As the ant tries to rejoin its colony, it feels a deep longing for the spider's companionship

Chapter 6: A New Family

6.1 A Surprising Reunion

- The ant hears a familiar voice—it's the spider, who couldn't leave the ant behind
- The spider admits it's come to care for the ant as its own

6.2 The Spider's Proposal

- The spider offers to adopt the ant, providing a new home where they can live together
- The ant, feeling torn between its old life and the new bond, considers the offer

6.3 Choosing Love

- The ant realizes that family is where love and care are, not just where you were born
- The ant chooses to stay with the spider, accepting the spider as its new parent

Chapter 7: Life in the Web

7.1 Adjusting to a New Home

- The ant settles into life with the spider, learning to live in the web
- They build a unique home that blends the spider's web with elements of the anthill

7.2 New Adventures

- o Together, the ant and spider explore the forest, making new friends and helping others
- o The ant and spider use their combined strengths to solve problems and protect their new family

7.3 A Happy Ending

- o The ant reflects on its journey, and the lessons learned about friendship, trust, and family
- o The story concludes with the ant and spider happily living together, proving that love knows no species

Chapter 3
Crafting Non-Fiction Narratives

Writing non-fiction is an art that requires both precision and creativity. While fiction allows writers to invent characters and scenarios, non-fiction demands a commitment to truth grounded in research and real-life experiences. Yet, like fiction, non-fiction also benefits from strong storytelling techniques that can engage readers and bring factual content to life.

The Art of Research: Methods, Using Quotes and Annotations, Fair Use

Research is the backbone of any non-fiction work. Whether you're writing a historical biography, a scientific essay, self-help, or a memoir, thorough and accurate research is crucial to establishing credibility and authority. The depth of your research will not only provide the factual foundation for your work but will also enrich your narrative, giving it texture and depth.

As I like to say – Get Nerdy with It! Speak from your own experience and wisdom. Don't make assumptions. Differentiate between fact and opinion.

1. Types of Research:

- **Primary** Sources are firsthand accounts or direct evidence of your topic, such as interviews, diaries, official documents, and original data. They are invaluable for bringing authenticity and a unique perspective to your writing.

- **Secondary Sources:** These include analyses, interpretations, or summaries of primary sources, like academic papers, books, and articles. Secondary sources help you understand the broader context of your subject and can provide additional insights and interpretations.

- **Using AI** is an acceptable tool for research. However, always check the information with at least two other sources. Yes, even AI gets it wrong – more often than you might expect. I like to use AI for definitions and to explain processes. It's a good starting point tool for outlining steps and researching locations, cultures, etc.

I once was asked to review a manuscript by an author who wanted to write a romance novel set on the Amalfi coast in a little town called Ravello. I have never actually been to this town, but I have been to Italy. So much of what this author had written seemed entirely out of character for Italy that I had to ask her if she had been to the place she's using as the backdrop in her book. She said no, but she assumed it would probably be a lot like her little town in Cape Cod, so she just used that as her "real" location and changed the name in the book to this town in Italy. I asked her why she didn't use her real town, or at least a city in New England, and she said she was worried people would figure out who she was talking about.

I bet you already know the problem with that. Not only were the characters NOT ITALIAN, but nothing they did, nothing they ate (they ate a lot of pasta, which she felt described them being Italian). The entire book made no sense. The story was good, but everything about reading the story felt off and out of place.

Had she either set the story in an area she knew- or at least done some research, her book might have been readable. This is the power of research.

2. Research Methods:

- **Library and Archival Research:** Libraries and archives are treasure troves of information, particularly for historical non-fiction. Don't overlook special collections, microfilm, and other resources that might be tucked away in less frequented sections.

- **Interviews:** Conducting interviews with experts or individuals with firsthand experience can add depth and personal perspective to your work. Prepare thoughtful questions and be open to unexpected insights.

- **Online Databases:** Accessing academic databases, government records, and credible websites can provide valuable data and research materials. However, always verify the credibility of your sources to avoid misinformation.

3. Organizing Your Research:

- Keep meticulous notes and organize them by themes, topics, or chapters. This will make it easier to reference your research as you write.

- Consider using research management tools or software to keep track of sources, quotes, and notes.

Using quotes from others in your book

Using quotes from others in your book can add credibility, depth, and variety to your writing. However, it's essential to use them appropriately and legally. Here's how you can effectively and ethically incorporate quotes into your book:

1. Relevance and Purpose

- **Choose Quotes Wisely:** Only use quotes that directly support or enhance your point. Ensure they are relevant to the topic or theme you are discussing.

- **Contextualize**: Introduce the quote and explain its significance to your argument or narrative. Don't just drop quotes into your text without integrating them into your writing.

2. Attribution

- **Cite the Source:** Always give proper credit to the original author. This typically involves mentioning the author's name, the work's title, and, if relevant, the publication date. For example:

    o According to the Author's Name in the Book Title (Year), "quote here."

- **Include Citations:** Depending on the style guide you're following (e.g., APA, MLA, Chicago), you may need to provide additional information, such as page numbers, in footnotes, endnotes, or a bibliography.

3. Fair Use Considerations

- **Length of the Quote**: The length of the quote can affect whether it falls under "fair use." Shorter quotes are generally more acceptable, while longer quotes may require permission from the copyright holder.

- **Purpose of Use:** Quotes used for criticism, commentary, education, or research are more likely to be considered fair use. However, even in these contexts, you should be mindful of the amount of text you're using.

- **Transformative Use:** If you're using the quote to transform the original work—such as using it for a new purpose, adding value, or providing commentary—you're more likely to fall under fair use.

4. Obtaining Permission

- **When to Seek Permission:** If you're using a long quote, a significant portion of a work, or if the material is central to your book, it's safer to seek permission from the copyright holder. This is especially important if the work is still under copyright (generally, works published after 1923).

- **How to Seek Permission:** Contact the publisher or rights holder of the work. Provide details about how you plan to use the quote, including the length, context, and purpose. Be prepared to pay a licensing fee if required.

5. Public Domain and Open Licenses

- **Public Domain:** Works published before 1923 or those where the copyright has expired are in the public domain, meaning you can use them without permission. Always verify the public domain status of a work before using it.

- **Creative Commons and Open Licenses:** Some works are available under open licenses like Creative Commons, which allow you to use the material under specific conditions, such as attribution or non-commercial use. Always check the terms of the license.

6. Editing and Paraphrasing

- **Paraphrase When Appropriate:** If the exact wording of a quote isn't necessary, consider paraphrasing the idea in your own words. Even when paraphrasing, you still need to credit the original author.

- **Accuracy is Key:** If you do use a quote, ensure it is accurate and not taken out of context. Misquoting can lead to misinterpretation and legal issues.

7. Ethical Considerations

- **Respectful Use:** Always consider the implications of using someone else's words. Ensure that the quote is used respectfully and ethically, particularly when quoting living individuals or works that address sensitive topics.

Example of Using a Quote in a Book:

- **Original Text:** "The only limit to our realization of tomorrow is our doubts of today." – Franklin D. Roosevelt.

- **In Your Book:** As Franklin D. Roosevelt once said, "The only limit to our realization of tomorrow is our doubts of today." This quote perfectly encapsulates the theme of overcoming fear that runs throughout this book.

Balancing Fact and Storytelling

While grounded in fact, nonfiction still benefits from storytelling techniques. The challenge lies in maintaining the integrity of the facts while crafting a narrative that captivates the reader. One of the things that is key to any non-fiction is sticking to the facts and letting your reader know when you are espousing an opinion. In this day and age, people seem to muddle the two. You gain more credibility by clarifying what is a fact – even if it's something you may not agree with what your opinion is, and, most importantly, why is that your opinion? Facts, especially in science, can evolve when more information is brought to light; perhaps you have something new to add to the information being used to state what is now considered fact. That's all well and good; however, if you continue to confuse the two, you may lose credibility with your reader. I have much more respect for and tend to listen to authors who understand the difference between fact and opinion and can clearly and concisely explain their position.

One other thing to consider is your reader – remember my 5 W's. I believe that, especially when writing about health and wellness, personal growth, and transformation, people are tired of the "guru on the stage"; they can also see through the malarkey rather quickly. Authentic vulnerability reaches people in a way that being the teacher or the know-it-all does not. If you take the time to write a book, be willing to leave a bit of yourself on the page so your readers will be as invested.

The Role of Narrative in Non-Fiction

Narrative elements such as plot, character development, and tension can be used to make factual content more compelling. For example, in a biography, you might highlight key moments in the subject's life that align with the traditional conflict and resolution narrative arc.

1. **Maintaining Accuracy:**

    - While it's tempting to embellish details for the sake of a better story, doing so can undermine the credibility of your work. Instead, look for ways to present facts in a way that is naturally engaging—through vivid descriptions, interesting anecdotes, and strong, clear writing.

2. **Ethical Considerations:**

    - Always consider the ethical implications of your narrative choices. Representing people, events, and information truthfully is not only a matter of credibility but also of respect for your subjects and your audience.

Using Personal Experience in Non-Fiction and Finding Your Voice

Drawing on personal experience can be one of the most powerful tools you have when writing non-fiction. It allows you to make a genuine connection with your readers, offering them a unique perspective that brings depth and authenticity to your narrative. Whether you're working on a memoir or weaving personal stories into other forms of non-fiction, remember my motto: stick to the facts, but don't be afraid to dive deep into your feelings about those facts.

When sharing personal stories, it's important to distinguish between the objective facts of what happened and your subjective experience of those events. You are entitled to your perspective, feelings, and opinions about any person, place, event, or moment in time. In fact, that's often what readers are most interested in: your unique viewpoint, your emotional journey, and how you navigated the challenges or choices you faced.

Think of it this way: your readers aren't just looking for a recount of events; they want to understand how those events affected you, how you made sense of them, and what you learned along the way. They're looking for insights and reflections that resonate with their own experiences, challenges, or dreams. They want to see themselves in your story and take away something that feels meaningful and relevant to their own lives.

Embracing Multiple Perspectives

One technique I find particularly helpful when writing about a significant experience is to explore the event from the perspective of others involved—even if I disagree with their viewpoint. This doesn't mean diluting your own story or apologizing for your feelings; rather, it's about adding depth and complexity to your narrative. By considering how others might have seen or felt about the same event, you can uncover layers of meaning and nuance that you might not have noticed before.

This approach does two things. First, it allows you to offer your readers a more well-rounded view of the situation, which can help them feel more engaged and invested in your story. Second, it can help you gain new insights into your own experiences. By stepping into someone else's shoes, even briefly, you might find yourself understanding your own emotions and actions in a new light. This can add richness to your narrative and make your writing more compelling.

Let's say you're writing about a falling out with a close friend. Instead of just recounting how hurt and betrayed you felt, you might take a moment to imagine what the experience was like for your friend. What pressures were they under? What fears or insecurities might have influenced their actions? Even if you still feel they were in the wrong, this exercise can help you articulate your story with greater empathy and complexity, which can make for a more engaging read.

Sharing Insights and Offering Value

When you write about personal experiences, especially those that had a significant impact on your life, you're often sharing hard-won wisdom. Readers come to non-fiction with the hope of learning something—about the world, about themselves, about the human condition. Your job is to help them find that wisdom by being open and honest about your own journey.

Think about the lessons you learned, the mistakes you made, and the breakthroughs you had. Be candid about your doubts, fears, and the moments when you didn't know what to do next. The more vulnerable and real you are, the more your readers will feel like they're on the journey with you.

But remember, sharing insights doesn't mean preaching or telling your readers what to do. It's about inviting them to reflect on their own lives by sharing the discoveries you've made in yours. For example, if you're writing about a time when you had to make a difficult decision, don't just focus on what choice you made; explore how you came to that decision, what you were afraid of, what you hoped for, and how it turned out. This approach can provide readers with tools and tips they can use in their own lives.

Navigating Emotional Terrain

Writing about personal experiences often means delving into emotional territory that can be challenging or even painful. It's natural to feel hesitant about revisiting difficult moments but remember that it's often these very experiences that hold the most potential for connection and growth.

When you write about an event that stirred strong emotions, take the time to explore those feelings in depth. What exactly were you feeling at that moment, and why? Was there fear, anger, sadness, or perhaps even a mix of emotions? How did those feelings change over time? How did they influence your actions and decisions?

Readers appreciate honesty and vulnerability. When you're willing to lay bare your emotions and admit to moments of doubt or weakness, you create a space for readers to do the same. It's in these moments of raw honesty that the strongest connections are made.

Balancing Honesty with Sensitivity

While it's important to be open and honest about your experiences, it's also crucial to be mindful of how your words might affect others, especially when writing about real people or sensitive situations. Striking the right balance between authenticity and respect can be tricky, but it's necessary.

If you're writing about an experience that involves others, consider how you frame their role in your story. Ask yourself whether you are being fair and accurate, and consider how your words might impact them. You don't need to hold back from telling your truth, but it's worth considering how you can do so in a way that is constructive rather than destructive. This approach not only respects others' privacy and perspectives but also adds credibility and integrity to your writing.

When you're writing non-fiction based on personal experience, you're entering into an implicit contract with your reader: you're promising to be honest and truthful, but you're also promising to treat the subjects of your story with care. This doesn't mean you have to sugarcoat or avoid difficult truths—it just means you approach your writing with empathy and understanding.

Creating a Dialogue with Your Reader

Ultimately, writing about personal experience creates a dialogue with your reader. It's not just about telling your story; it's about inviting your reader to see their own story reflected in yours. It's about finding common ground, sharing struggles and triumphs, and offering a hand to others on similar journeys.

Think of your writing as a conversation, not a monologue. Leave room for your readers to bring their own experiences and interpretations into the mix. Ask questions, share doubts, and be open about the things you're still figuring out. This openness creates a sense of partnership between you and your reader, making your writing feel like an ongoing exchange rather than a one-sided lecture.

Finding Your Own Voice

Finally, remember that writing about personal experience is as much about finding your voice as it is about telling your story. Your voice is what makes your writing unique; it's the lens through which you see the world, the way you express your thoughts, and the rhythm of your words. Don't be afraid to let that voice come through, even if it feels vulnerable or raw.

Your readers are coming to you because they want to hear your perspective. They want to know how you see the world and how you make sense of your experiences. So be yourself, be honest, and trust that your voice is enough.

1. Relevance to the Subject:

- Use personal experiences that are directly relevant to the topic at hand. Your experiences should enhance the reader's understanding of the subject, not detract from it.

2. Balancing Personal and Universal:

- While personal stories can be compelling, balancing them with universal themes and broader insights is important. Aim to relate your personal experience to the reader's own life or to a wider context.

3. Vulnerability and Authenticity:

- Writing about personal experiences often requires vulnerability. Authenticity is key; readers can usually tell when a story feels forced or inauthentic. Embrace the messiness of real life, and don't be afraid to show your true self.

4. Avoiding Self-Indulgence:

- Be cautious of self-indulgence. While it's important to share personal insights, ensure that they serve the narrative and are not just included for the sake of self-expression. The focus should remain on what will be most engaging and meaningful to the reader.

Chapter 4
Writing Techniques

It may feel like there are a lot of steps in this process, and you haven't even begun writing yet! Trust me when I tell you that these steps are crucial to completing your book and crafting a rich and captivating story that will engage your readers on a level you could only hope for.

The "Devil is in the details," as they say, and now that you have completed digging deep into all the nooks and crannies of your creative heart and soul, you know your reader, you know your characters and their journey, you have probably uncovered more juicy tidbits to your story than you had originally thought existed.

Even for my clients who write nonfiction, these tools have transformed their ideas into the compelling and transformative books they hoped to write.

This is the work that elevates your writing. It may not seem "creative" or fun initially, but the more you embrace the process, the more excited you will be about writing it.

The steps you just read are the ones many authors, who don't finish their book skip. This is why writers write multiple drafts and get lost down a rabbit hole of revisions.

Now that you have done the work let's get writing!

There is much to consider as you sit down to write your book. The following tips and tools do not represent the "right" way. You've got to find your own voice, your own groove to your writing style.

One thing to consider: writing is different from journaling. Journaling is an excellent tool for "vomiting on the page"—if you will—your feelings, thoughts, and even specific ideas and thoughts you want to remember. Journaling often doesn't have the structure or thoughtfulness one undertakes when writing out your story or ideas for anyone else to read.

Sometimes, I like to record myself telling the story or explaining the concept. Then, I transcribe that recording, which provides the basis for my piece. Often, when we share something verbally, we aren't staring at a blank page worried about the right word, and we add details and insights we might forget if we're "trying to write."

This is a great tool; however, it's not a replacement for writing, editing, and organizing your work into a readable structure.

Helpful tips and tools to consider as you write your book:

Mastering Dialogue

Dialogue is one of the most powerful tools in a writer's arsenal. It brings characters to life, advances the plot, and reveals essential information about the story and its participants. Effective dialogue is more than just characters speaking—it's about creating conversations that feel real and serve a purpose.

1. Purposeful Dialogue:

- **Advance the Plot:** Dialogue should move the story forward. Each conversation should have a purpose, whether revealing key information, building tension, or showing character development.
- **Reveal Character:** How a character speaks—tone, choice of words, and mannerisms—reveals much about their personality, background, and emotional state. Use dialogue to show who your characters are.

2. Realistic Speech:

- **Avoid Overly Formal Language:** Real people don't speak in perfectly constructed sentences. Incorporate natural pauses, interruptions, and colloquialisms to make dialogue feel authentic.
- **Balance Realism with Readability:** While you want dialogue to sound natural, it's also important that it's straightforward and easy to follow. Avoid the exact replication of real-life speech patterns, which can include too many ums, ahhs, and unfinished thoughts.

3. Dialogue Tags and Beats:

- **Use Tags Sparingly:** Dialogue tags like "he said" or "she asked" should clarify who is speaking but should not overwhelm the dialogue itself. Use action beats (e.g., "She sipped her coffee") to show who is speaking and what they're doing without relying too heavily on tags.

- **Avoid Overly Descriptive Tags:** Tags like "he exclaimed" or "she interjected" can feel forced. A simple "said" is often enough, letting the dialogue and action convey the tone.

Show vs. Tell

"Show, don't tell" is a fundamental writing principle that encourages writers to allow readers to experience the story through action, senses, and feelings rather than through exposition and summary.

1. The Power of Showing:

- **Engage the Senses:** Instead of telling the reader that a character is angry, show their clenched fists, their reddening face, and the sharpness in their voice. This approach helps readers feel and visualize the emotions and actions, making the experience more vivid.

- **Create Immersive Scenes:** Showing creates a more immersive and engaging narrative. For example, instead of saying that the room was messy, describe the crumpled papers on the floor, the coffee stains on the desk, and the overflowing trash can.

2. When to Tell:

- **Exposition:** Sometimes, telling is necessary, especially when conveying background information or moving the story along quickly. The key is to use telling strategically and sparingly, ensuring it doesn't disrupt the narrative flow.

- **Pacing:** Telling can be useful for pacing, allowing the story to quickly move through less critical moments while reserving showing for more significant scenes.

3. Balancing Show and Tell:

- A good story typically balances showing and telling. Use showing for key moments, character development, and emotional scenes while using telling for transitions, background information, or when the specifics are less important.

Using Descriptive Writing

Descriptive writing is the heartbeat of storytelling—the brushstrokes that bring worlds and characters to life in the minds of your readers. Every great book you've read has mastered a balance between vivid description and concise storytelling. Interestingly, younger generations, like Millennials and Gen Z, often prefer a more streamlined approach to description. They want you to get to the point, much like a good movie does. Notice how a film can set an entire scene with just a few shots, giving you everything you need to know in seconds. That's the mindset you want to bring into your writing: be descriptive but make sure every detail serves a purpose.

When describing something, ask yourself: does this matter to the story or the character? Don't tell me about a character's shoes unless those shoes tell me something important. Maybe they're scuffed and worn, hinting at an arduous journey or a rough past. Or perhaps they're pristine in a chaotic setting, suggesting something unexpected about the character. This is where all the work you've put into your character breakdowns comes into play. Use the background and personality you've created to guide your descriptive choices, ensuring they add depth and insight rather than filler.

Pro Tip: Watch Out for Overused Words

Keep an eye on words like "really," "actually," "literally," and other similar fillers. They often sneak into our writing and clutter up the prose without adding much value. We all have that one word we tend to overuse—set yourself a challenge: use it once, and then be done with it unless it's absolutely essential to your narrative.

Think of your descriptions like seasoning in a dish: too little and the flavor will fall flat; too much and it will overwhelm the taste. Find that perfect balance, and you'll create a rich, immersive story without losing its pace or purpose.

1. Vivid Imagery:

- **Use the Senses:** Engage the senses in your descriptions. What does a scene look, sound, smell, taste, and feel like? Using sensory details creates a more immersive experience for the reader.

- **Specificity Over Generalization:** Specific details are more effective than vague descriptions. Instead of saying, "The garden was beautiful," describe the "vibrant roses in full bloom, their petals glowing red in the morning sun."

2. Similes and Metaphors:

- **Enhance Descriptions:** Similes and metaphors can add layers of meaning and create powerful imagery. For example, "Her smile was as bright as the summer sun" or "The night was a velvet blanket covering the earth."

- **Avoid Clichés:** While similes and metaphors are effective, avoid overused expressions. Fresh, original comparisons will have a greater impact.

3. Balance Description with Action:

- **Pace Your Descriptions:** Too much description can slow the pace of your story. Balance descriptive passages with action and dialogue to maintain momentum and keep the reader engaged.

-

Writing with Authenticity

Authenticity in writing is about being true to your voice, characters, and subject matter. It's about writing with honesty and integrity, allowing your genuine perspective and emotions to shine through. For memoirs and nonfiction, write what you know to be true, and regardless, use your research, your Hero's Journey, your character breakdowns, and your beat sheet so you don't lose the plot. This is precisely why you did all that work in the first place.

1. Honest Emotions:

- **Write from the Heart:** Don't shy away from expressing raw, honest emotions in your writing. Authenticity resonates with readers because it reflects the complexity and truth of the human experience.

- **Avoid Forced Drama:** Authentic writing is more potent than contrived or exaggerated emotions. Let the emotion arise naturally from the situation and characters.

2. Staying True to Your Characters:

- **Character Consistency:** Ensure that your characters act and speak in ways that are consistent with their background, personality, and motivations. Authentic characters behave in ways that feel real, even when faced with extraordinary circumstances.

- **Voice and Perspective:** Write in a way that is true to your characters' voices. Avoid imposing your own thoughts and feelings on them unless it aligns with their established personality.

3. Authentic Themes and Messages:

- **Write What You Believe:** The themes and messages in your writing should reflect your own beliefs and perspectives. Authentic writing comes from a place of truth and conviction.

- **Avoid Preachiness:** While conveying your message is important, avoid being overly didactic. Trust your readers to draw their own conclusions based on the story and characters you've presented.

Developing Your Voice

Your writing voice is your unique style, the way your personality comes through in your writing. Developing a strong, distinctive voice is key to standing out as a writer and connecting with your audience.

1. Finding Your Voice:

- **Experiment:** Try writing in different styles, genres, and perspectives to discover what feels most natural to you.

- **Write Regularly:** The more you write, the more your voice will develop. Writing regularly helps you refine your style and gain confidence in your voice.

2. Consistency in Voice:

- **Maintain Your Style:** While being versatile is important, consistency in your voice helps create a cohesive narrative. Your readers should be able to recognize your voice throughout your work, even if the subject matter changes.

- **Adapt but Don't Compromise:** While your voice should be adaptable to different genres or audiences, don't compromise its authenticity. Your voice is what makes your writing unique, and it's important to stay true to it.

3. Embrace Your Uniqueness:

- **Celebrate Your Individuality:** Your voice reflects your unique perspective and experiences. Don't try to fit into a mold—embrace what makes your writing different, whether it's your tone, humor, rhythm, or choice of words.

- **Confidence**: Trust in your voice. The more you write with confidence, the more your voice will shine through, making your work more engaging and authentic.

Forward, Preface, and Introduction

What Are They and Do You Need Them?

When writing a book, especially in non-fiction, you might consider including sections like a foreword, preface, and introduction. These components serve specific purposes and can enhance the reader's understanding and engagement with your work. However, depending on your book's content and goals, you may not need all of them. Here's an explanation of each and guidance on when you might choose to include them.

1. Foreword

What It Is: A foreword is a short section written by someone other than the author, usually someone of note or authority in the book's subject area. The foreword typically appears before the preface and introduction.

Purpose:

- **Credibility and Endorsement:** The primary purpose of a foreword is to lend credibility and authority to the book. When a respected figure in your field writes the foreword, it serves as an endorsement, helping to attract readers who trust the foreword writer's opinion.

- **Context**: The foreword often provides context for the book, explaining why the subject is important and why the author is particularly suited to write about it.

- Personal Connection: The foreword writer might share how they know the author, why they were drawn to the book, or what they personally gained from it.

Do You Need It?

- Yes, if You can secure a foreword from a well-known or respected individual in your field who can add significant value to your book through their endorsement.

- No, if you don't have access to someone who can provide a meaningful foreword or if your book's content stands strong without additional endorsement,

2. Preface

What It Is: A preface is written by the author and provides an opportunity to speak directly to the reader about the book's creation. It usually comes after the foreword (if one is included) and before the introduction.

Purpose:

- **Background Information:** The preface allows the author to share the story behind the book—what inspired it, how it came to be, and any challenges faced during the writing process.

- **Author's Motivation:** It can explain why the author felt compelled to write the book and what they hope to achieve.

- **Acknowledgments:** The preface often includes acknowledgments of people who contributed to the book's development, whether through research, feedback, or support.

Do You Need It?

- Yes, if You want to provide readers with insight into your personal journey as the author or feel that understanding the book's background will enrich the reader's experience.

- No, if The book's content speaks for itself, and the reader doesn't need additional context to appreciate the material.

3. Introduction

What It Is: The introduction is a section written by the author that directly addresses the reader and offers an overview of what to expect in the book. It's typically more content-focused than the preface.

Purpose:

- **Overview of the Book:** The introduction outlines the book's main themes, arguments, or narrative. It often provides a roadmap of what the reader can expect in the following chapters.

- **Setting the Stage:** It helps to set the stage for the reader, offering necessary context or background information to help them understand the book's content.

- **Engaging the Reader:** A strong introduction grabs the reader's attention and motivates them to continue reading by clearly stating the value they will gain from the book.

Do You Need It?

- Yes, if your book is complex and readers would benefit from an overview, if you need to establish context, or if you need to explain how to approach the book's content.

- No, if the book's structure is straightforward and doesn't require additional explanation or if you prefer to dive straight into the content without preliminary discussion.

Deciding What You Need

- **Foreword**: Include it if you can secure a strong endorsement that will enhance the book's credibility.

- **Preface**: Use it if you want to share personal insights or background information that might deepen the reader's connection to the book.

- **Introduction**: Include it if you need to provide context, an overview, or a guide to help the reader navigate your book.

Prologue and Epilogue: What Are They and Do You Need Them in Fiction?

In fiction, a prologue and an epilogue serve specific purposes that can enhance your storytelling. However, whether or not you need them depends on the structure of your narrative and what you aim to achieve with your story. Here's an explanation of each and advice on when you might consider using them.

1. Prologue

What It Is: A prologue is an introductory section of a book that precedes the main story. It typically provides background information, sets the tone, or presents a scene that is crucial to understanding the rest of the narrative. The prologue is often set in a different time or place than the story's main events.

Purpose:

- **Background Information:** A prologue can introduce backstory or important events that happened before the book's main timeline, which the reader needs to know to fully understand the story.

- **Foreshadowing**: It can be used to foreshadow key events or themes that will unfold later in the story, creating suspense or intrigue.

- **Setting the Tone:** The prologue can establish the tone or mood of the book, helping the reader get a sense of what to expect.

- **Introducing the Villain or Conflict:** In some genres, such as thrillers or fantasy, a prologue might introduce the antagonist or central conflict, setting up the stakes for the protagonist.

Do You Need It?

- Yes, if There's essential information that the reader must know before the main story begins or if you want to create a hook that draws readers in right from the start. It's also helpful if you're dealing with complex world-building or wish to create a mystery or tension that will carry through the narrative.

- No, if the backstory or crucial details can be seamlessly integrated into the main narrative or if the prologue might delay the reader's immersion into the central plot. Some readers tend to skip prologues, so if the information isn't critical, it might be better to start with the first chapter.

2. Epilogue

What It Is: An epilogue is a book's concluding section that comes after the main story has ended. It's often used to provide closure, show the aftermath of the story's events, or give a glimpse into the future of the characters.

Purpose:

- **Providing Closure:** An epilogue can tie up loose ends and address the reader's lingering questions after the story's climax.

- **Showing the Future:** It can provide a look into the characters' lives after the events of the book, showing how they've changed or what their future holds.

- **Offering Reflection:** The epilogue can offer a reflective perspective, allowing characters or the narrator to ponder the significance of the story's events.

- **Sequel Setup:** In series fiction, an epilogue might hint at what's to come in the next book, setting up new conflicts or mysteries.

Do You Need It?

- Yes, if You want to offer a satisfying conclusion that goes beyond the final chapter, providing the reader with additional insight or closure. It's also useful if your story is part of a series and you want to create anticipation for the next installment.

- No, if the story concludes naturally in the final chapter, with all plot threads resolved and no need for further explanation. If the epilogue feels like an unnecessary add-on rather than a meaningful part of the narrative, it might be better to leave it out.

Deciding What You Need

- Prologue: Consider including a prologue if it adds essential context, builds suspense, **or enhan**ces the reader's understanding of the story from the outset. Ensure it's engaging and directly relevant to the main narrative.

- **Epilogue**: Use an epilogue if it provides meaningful closure, offers a satisfying glimpse into the characters' futures, or sets up a sequel. Make sure it enhances the reader's experience rather than merely extending the story.

In fiction, both the prologue and epilogue can be powerful tools when used effectively, but they are by no means mandatory. The key is to ensure that these sections serve a clear purpose and enrich the overall storytelling experience. If they feel like necessary extensions of your story, include them. If not, it's perfectly fine to let your narrative begin and end with the main chapters.

Chapter 5
Overcoming Writer's Block

Guess what, remember the Hero's Journey? Well, the moment you received the call to write your book, your journey began. At some point, you're going to enter the dark night of the soul (entering the innermost cave/surviving the ordeal, 7-8). Sometimes, this is referred to as writer's block. It's that moment when the words don't flow, the ideas seem to evaporate, and the once-clear path forward becomes obscured. Writer's block can be a temporary hurdle or a prolonged challenge, but it's important to recognize that it is not insurmountable; it's part of the process.

Common Causes of Writer's Block

Understanding the root causes of writer's block is the first step in overcoming it. While the experience is highly individual, several common factors can contribute to this creative obstacle:

1. **Perfectionism**: Many writers struggle with the pressure to produce flawless work. The fear of not meeting high standards can paralyze creativity, leading to self-doubt and hesitation to even begin writing.

2. **Fear of Failure:** Closely related to perfectionism, the fear of failure can stop a writer in their tracks. The worry that their work won't be good enough or that it will be criticized can make the task of writing seem daunting.

3. **Lack of Inspiration:** Sometimes, writer's block arises simply because inspiration is lacking. Whether it's a dry spell in creativity or difficulty in connecting with the subject matter, the absence of inspiration can make writing feel like an uphill battle.

4. **Burnout**: Writing, especially under tight deadlines or pressure, can lead to burnout. When a writer is mentally or physically exhausted, it becomes nearly impossible to produce quality work, leading to a cycle of frustration and blockage.

5. **Life Distractions:** External factors such as personal issues, work responsibilities, or environmental changes can create distractions that interfere with a writer's ability to focus on their craft.

Practical Strategies for Breaking Through

Here are some tools for moving through your dark night of the soul and reaping the rewards.

1. **Set Small, Achievable Goals:** Breaking down your writing tasks into smaller, manageable goals can make the process less intimidating. Instead of aiming to write an entire chapter, focus on completing a single paragraph or page. This approach can help you build momentum and reduce the pressure to be perfect from the start. This is why you did the pre-work to your writing. If you've done that work, this part should flow easier (not easily fyi)

2. **Free Writing/Journaling:** One of the most effective ways to break through writer's block is to engage in free writing. Set a timer for 10-15 minutes and write without stopping or censoring yourself. The goal is not to produce polished work but to get your creative juices flowing. Often, this exercise can help uncover new ideas or solutions to problems in your writing. Even writing about why you don't want to write will shift things for you.

3. **Change Your Environment:** Sometimes, a change of scenery can do wonders for your creativity. If you're feeling stuck, try writing in a different location—a park, a café, or even a different room in your home. The new environment can stimulate your senses and provide a fresh perspective.

4. **Read and Seek Inspiration:** Reading other works—whether books, articles, or poetry—can serve as a source of inspiration. Exposing yourself to different styles, genres, and ideas can spark your own creativity and help you overcome the mental block.

5. **Set a Routine:** Establishing a regular writing routine can help train your brain to write at certain times, reducing the likelihood of blockages. Even if you're not feeling particularly inspired, sitting down to write at the same time each day can help make writing a habit rather than a chore.

6. **Talk It Out:** Discussing your writing project with a friend, fellow writer, or mentor can provide valuable insights and new ideas. Or, as I suggested earlier, record

yourself as if you're speaking to a dear friend or trusted colleague. Sometimes, verbalizing your thoughts can help clarify your ideas and reignite your passion for the project.

7. **Accept Imperfection:** First drafts are not meant to be perfect. Allow yourself to write poorly, knowing that revision is part of the process. By lowering the stakes and accepting that not every word has to be perfect, you free yourself from the paralyzing grip of perfectionism.

8. **Ask your cosmic co-writer:** Take a nap, take a walk, meditate, and have a conversation with BoB!

Sustaining Creativity and Motivation

Overcoming writer's block is just the first step. Sustaining creativity and motivation over the long term is essential for any writer. Here are some strategies to keep your creative energy high:

1. **Set Long-Term Goals:** Having clear, long-term goals for your writing can help keep you motivated. Whether it's finishing a novel, publishing an article, or completing a blog series, knowing what you're working towards can provide the necessary drive to keep going.

2. **Practice Mindfulness and Self-Care:** Writing is a mental exercise; like any exercise, it requires energy and focus. Incorporating mindfulness practices such as meditation, deep breathing, or even taking regular breaks can help keep your mind clear and creative. Additionally, maintaining a healthy work-life balance, getting enough sleep, and staying physically active can all contribute to sustained creativity.

3. **Celebrate Small Wins:** Writing is a journey, and it's important to acknowledge and celebrate the small victories along the way. Whether it's finishing a chapter, hitting a word count milestone, or receiving positive feedback, these moments of success can motivate you to keep moving forward.

4. **Stay Curious and Open:** Curiosity is a powerful driver of creativity. Stay open to new experiences, ideas, and perspectives. Engage with different art forms, cultures, and people. The more you feed your mind with diverse stimuli, the richer your creative output will be.

5. **Join a Writing Community:** Being part of a writing community—whether online or in-person—can provide support, encouragement, and inspiration. Sharing your work, receiving feedback, and connecting with other writers can help sustain your motivation and keep you accountable.

Most importantly, don't worry or beat yourself up about taking a break from writing. BoB (my nickname for the Universe, God, and Source) sometimes has a plan that we aren't aware of. Walking away for a day, a week, or even a few years might be just what your manuscript needs.

I began writing Killing Buddha as a screenplay almost 20 years ago, had it all set up, and was ready to start filming when catastrophe struck and I lost my lead actress. When I thought all was lost, I was offered a book deal for Tipping Sacred Cows from Simon and Schuster. I wrote that book, learned a lot about writing and publishing, and eventually, Killing Buddha evolved from a screenplay into a book, which, if I do say so myself, became a much better piece of work and is now evolving into a series. Timing is everything; I believe now is a better time for that project to emerge.

All this is to say, be patient with yourself, trust the process, and listen to your gut.

Part 2:
Polishing Your Manuscript

You set a goal to finish your manuscript in the beginning. Using the process I've outlined in the above chapters and having a committed writing schedule of about four to six hours a week, you can finish your first draft in about four to six months.

The main reason people do not finish their manuscripts is because they do not fully commit to it. They find all the reasons in the world not to sit down and write. It's okay, no judgment – it happens to all of us.

However, if you have done the work spiritually, mentally, and physically and followed the process, now you have a first draft of your book.

Many people make their biggest mistake right here.

They fall in love with their manuscript and miss all the red flags.

I can't tell you how many times I have been contacted by a writer who thinks they need a "basic" edit when what they really need is an editor.

If you have followed my process, usually your manuscript is in pretty good shape, but don't be fooled into thinking you don't need an editor or that your friend read it and liked it, so it must be good to go. FYI- your friends aren't telling you the truth. They might have some constructive feedback, but you still need an editor.

Writing and publishing a book is not a small endeavor. It takes time and money. Even if you get a publisher, you should be prepared to support your book financially.

If you get a publisher, they will likely pay for an editor to work with you on your book. However, with that being said, you should always put your best foot forward, and it's a good idea to have someone who is a professional review whatever you submit.

If you intend to self-publish your book, take your time with the editing process. A good editor costs a minimum of $8,000-$10,000. You can find some who charge less, but buyer beware.

Your time is valuable, and your credibility as a writer is on the line. Like the woman who wanted to write a book about herself and then pretended she was Italian, take the time to do the work on your manuscript, get it in the best shape you can, and then ask for and be prepared to pay for the help needed to deliver a quality, professionally produced book.

Chapter 6
The Art of Revision

Self-Editing Techniques

Revision is where the true magic of writing happens. In this phase, you shape your raw ideas into a coherent, polished piece of work. While the initial draft is about getting your thoughts down on paper, revision is about refining those thoughts, enhancing clarity, and ensuring that your message resonates with your readers.

Big Picture Revisions: The first step in self-editing involves looking at the big picture. This is where you examine the overall structure and flow of your work. Start by setting your manuscript aside for a few days or even weeks. This break allows you to return to your writing with fresh eyes and a more objective perspective.

When you revisit your manuscript, read through it in its entirety without making any changes. This will feel almost impossible – but give it your best. I like to make notes of what I find that needs revisions and keep moving forward in my review. This read-through is crucial for identifying major structural issues. Ask yourself questions like:

- Does the story or argument progress logically from beginning to end?
- Are the main points or themes clear and well-developed?
- Are there any sections that feel out of place, redundant, or unnecessary?
- Is the pacing consistent, or are there parts that drag or move too quickly?

This revision stage is about ensuring that your manuscript has a solid foundation. It's where you might decide to reorder chapters, combine or split sections, or even cut entire scenes or arguments that don't serve the overall purpose of the work.

Paragraph and Sentence-Level Revisions: Once you've addressed the larger structural elements, it's time to zoom in on the details. Paragraph-level revisions involve ensuring that each paragraph contributes to the development of your ideas or story. Each paragraph should have a clear purpose, whether it's to introduce a new concept, develop a point, or provide a transition between sections.

At the sentence level, focus on clarity and conciseness. Look for sentences that are overly complex or convoluted and break them down into simpler, more direct language. Pay attention to the rhythm and flow of your sentences—vary sentence length to create a natural cadence that keeps readers engaged.

Eliminate unnecessary words and phrases that don't add value to your writing. For example, instead of saying, "due to the fact that," you can say "because." These small changes can significantly improve the readability of your work.

AI and other editing and writing tools

Using AI and Other Writing Tools

This is where some AI tools become helpful. Here are the top three highly recommended AI editing tools:

Grammarly

- **Overview:** Grammarly is a comprehensive writing assistant that helps with grammar, punctuation, style, and tone. It's available as a web app, browser extension, and desktop app, making it accessible across different platforms.

- **Features:**

    o **Grammar and Punctuation Checks:** Grammarly identifies and suggests corrections for common errors, including subject-verb agreement, incorrect punctuation, and sentence fragments.

    o **Style and Clarity Suggestions:** It offers suggestions to improve sentence structure, clarity, and conciseness.

    o **Tone Detector:** Grammarly provides feedback on the tone of your writing, helping ensure that it matches your intended message.

    o **Plagiarism Detection:** It includes a plagiarism checker that compares your text against billions of web pages.

- **Best For:** Writers looking for a comprehensive tool that improves both technical accuracy and overall readability.

2. ProWritingAid

- **Overview**: ProWritingAid is a powerful editing tool that combines grammar and style checking with in-depth reports to help writers improve their craft. It's known for its detailed feedback and educational approach.

- **Features:**
    - Grammar and Style Checks: Like Grammarly, ProWritingAid corrects grammar and punctuation errors and offers style suggestions.
    - Detailed Reports: It provides over 20 different reports on aspects like overused words, sentence length variation, readability, and more.
    - In-Depth Analysis: The tool analyzes your writing and offers suggestions to improve pacing, repetition, dialogue, and consistency.
    - Integrations: ProWritingAid integrates with Scrivener, Google Docs, Word, and other popular writing tools.

- **Best For:** Writers who want a deep dive into their writing with detailed feedback and educational insights.

3. Hemingway Editor

- **Overview**: Hemingway Editor is a straightforward tool designed to make your writing clear and concise. It focuses on readability and style, helping you craft direct, impactful prose.

- **Features**:
    - Readability Score: Hemingway assigns a readability grade level to your text, encouraging you to simplify complex sentences.
    - Highlighting: The tool highlights passive voice, adverbs, complex phrases, and hard-to-read sentences, making it easy to spot and correct.
    - Simple Interface: Hemingway's minimalist interface helps writers focus on improving their text without distractions.

- **Best For:** Writers looking to simplify their writing and improve clarity, particularly in non-fiction and content writing.

Each tool has its strengths, and many writers find it helpful to use a combination of them depending on their project's specific needs.

A word of caution. AI doesn't always get it right. Take the time to review every suggestion. I often find that AI tools tend to change my voice. For instance, passive writing isn't always a bad thing. Review each suggestion carefully and decide if it works for you. You will have a chance (or at least I hope you choose to) to work with a professional editor who will further edit the work, so if it doesn't feel right, don't change it.

Common Pitfalls to Watch For:

- **Passive Voice:** While passive voice isn't always wrong, it can make your writing less direct and more difficult to follow. Consider whether an active voice might be more effective in conveying your message.

- **Overused Words:** Every writer has words or phrases they tend to overuse, such as "really, literally, actually," etc. These can dilute the impact of your writing. Tools like word processors or online editors can help you identify and address these overused words.

- **Consistency:** Ensure consistency in your narrative voice, tense, and point of view. Inconsistencies can confuse readers and disrupt the flow of your story or argument.

Reading Aloud: One of the most powerful self-editing techniques is reading your work aloud. When you read aloud, you engage your auditory senses, which can help you catch errors your eyes might skim over. Awkward phrasings, run-on sentences, and missing words often become more apparent when you hear them. Additionally, reading aloud helps you gauge the natural rhythm of your prose and can reveal where the writing may need smoothing or clarification.

Taking a Break: After completing a round of self-editing, consider taking another break before revisiting your manuscript. This pause can help you detach further from your work, allowing you to approach it with an even more critical eye. Writing and revising are both intense mental processes, and giving yourself time between rounds of revision can lead to more thoughtful and effective edits.

Working with Beta Readers

After your initial round of self-editing, it's time to introduce fresh perspectives into the revision process. Beta readers play a crucial role in this phase—they offer an outside view of your work, helping you see issues you might have missed.

Beta readers are not your friends, mom, brother, or sister unless they fit your target audience, are willing to read objectively, and give you honest, constructive feedback. Just because they "like it" isn't a reason to say your book is done.

You can find Beta readers through writing groups on social media or even in your hometown.

Choosing Beta Readers: Selecting the right beta readers is critical to getting valuable feedback. Your beta readers should represent a cross-section of your target audience. They should be genuinely interested in your genre or topic and be willing to provide honest, constructive feedback. However, diversity in your beta readers is equally important. A variety of perspectives can highlight different aspects of your manuscript that need attention.

Consider including a mix of people, such as:

- Avid readers of your genre who can offer insights into how your work compares to others in the field.

- Writers or editors who can provide feedback on technical aspects of your writing.

- Individuals with a background in the subject matter of your book who can help ensure accuracy and depth in your content.

Guiding the Feedback: To make the most of your beta readers' input, provide them with a framework for their feedback. This can be in the form of specific questions or areas you want them to focus on. For example:

- Are the characters well-developed and relatable?

- Is the story's pacing appropriate, or does it drag in certain sections?

- Are there any plot points or arguments that are confusing or unclear?

- Does the dialogue sound natural and contribute to character development?

Providing a questionnaire or a feedback form can help focus their responses and ensure you receive actionable insights. However, also encourage them to share any thoughts or reactions that fall outside these guidelines, as unexpected observations can be incredibly valuable.

Receiving and Working with Feedback – Self-Editing

When the feedback starts rolling in, it's natural to feel a mix of emotions—excitement, anxiety, and even defensiveness. Remember that criticism of your work is not criticism of you. Each piece of feedback is a tool you can use to improve your manuscript.

Start by reading through all the feedback without making any immediate changes. Note recurring themes or suggestions, as these often point to areas that multiple readers found problematic. Consider creating a feedback summary sheet where you compile the key points from each beta reader, making it easier to spot patterns.

Not all feedback will align with your vision for the book, and that's okay. Your job is to discern which suggestions will help you achieve your goals and which might detract from your intended message or story. Trust your instincts, but also be open to revising parts of your manuscript that you might feel attached to if doing so will strengthen the overall work.

Incorporating Feedback: Incorporating feedback can be daunting, especially when it involves significant changes. Approach this task methodically:

- Prioritize major issues first, such as plot holes, character inconsistencies, or unclear arguments. Addressing these larger concerns will often lead to more cohesive revisions.

- Once the major issues are resolved, move on to smaller, more detailed feedback, such as tightening up dialogue, improving descriptions, or correcting minor factual inaccuracies.

Remember that revision is an iterative process. You may need to go through several rounds of revisions, each time honing your manuscript further. It can be helpful to share revised sections with your beta readers or a trusted critique partner to ensure the changes are working as intended.

The Role of Feedback in the Revision Process

Feedback is a crucial component of the revision process. It allows you to step outside of your own perspective and see your work through the eyes of others. However, receiving feedback can be challenging, especially when it highlights areas of your writing that need significant revision.

Emotional Preparation: Before you even receive feedback, it's important to prepare yourself emotionally. Understand that feedback is meant to help you improve, not to criticize you personally. Feeling defensive or upset about critiques is normal, especially if you've invested a lot of time and energy into your work. Acknowledge these feelings, but don't let them cloud your judgment.

Analyzing Feedback: When you receive feedback, start by reading through it carefully and without making any immediate changes. This step is crucial for gaining a clear understanding of what your beta readers or editors are trying to convey. Take notes as you read, jotting down any initial reactions or thoughts you have about the feedback.

Next, categorize the feedback into different types:

- **Structural Feedback:** Comments that pertain to the overall structure, such as plot issues, pacing problems, or organization of ideas.

- **Character/Argument Development:** Feedback that addresses the depth and development of your characters or the clarity and persuasiveness of your arguments.

- **Stylistic Feedback:** Notes on your writing style, including voice, tone, and language use.

- **Technical Feedback:** Corrections of grammar, spelling, punctuation, or factual inaccuracies.

By categorizing the feedback, you can approach the revision process more organized and focused. This method also helps you prioritize the changes that need to be made, starting with the most critical issues.

Balancing Feedback with Your Vision: One of the challenges of the revision process is balancing your own vision with the feedback you receive. While it's important to be open to suggestions, you must also maintain the integrity of your original vision.

Ask yourself the following questions as you evaluate each piece of feedback:

- Does this feedback align with my goals for the manuscript?

- Will making this change enhance the clarity or impact of my writing?

- Is the feedback addressing an issue I needed clarification on?

If the answer to these questions is yes, then it's worth considering the suggested revisions. However, if a piece of feedback feels off or doesn't resonate with your vision, it's okay to set it aside. Remember, you are the author, and ultimately, the decisions about your manuscript are yours to make.

Implementing Feedback: Once you've decided which feedback to act on, start by revisiting your beat sheet, character breakdowns, and other research you created in the early part of your process. You can add the notes to your outline using a different color and create a revision plan or checklist to keep track of the changes you need to make.

Once you've organized what you plan on reworking, begin with the most significant revisions and work your way down to smaller tweaks.

Chapter 7
Professional Editing

Writing a book is an enormous accomplishment, but the journey doesn't end when you finish your first draft. Professional editing is crucial to bring your manuscript to its fullest potential. Unfortunately, it is a step most new writers try to skip. As mentioned, this process will elevate your writing if engaged properly.

You've already considered how you want your book published. If you desire to be published by a publisher, you may have the opportunity to work with an editor provided by the publisher. Depending on the size of the publisher, they sometimes prefer to have their chosen editors work with their authors. Later in this book, we will review how to approach editors and literary agents with your book proposal. Regardless, understanding how to work with an editor remains the same, whether it's an in-house editor or one you hire directly.

Types of Editing: Developmental, Copyediting, Proofreading

Understanding the different types of editing is crucial for determining what your manuscript needs at various stages of development. Professional editing typically involves three main types: developmental editing, copyediting, and proofreading.

Developmental Editing: Developmental editing, or substantive or structural editing, is the most comprehensive form of editing. It focuses on the big-picture elements of your manuscript, such as structure, plot, character development, pacing, and overall cohesiveness.

- **Structure**: The editor examines the structure of your manuscript, looking at the order and flow of chapters and scenes. They ensure that your narrative or argument progresses logically and that each part contributes to the overall story or message.

- **Plot and Character Development:** For fiction, the editor will assess the strength of your plot and the depth of your characters. They might suggest adding, removing, or rearranging scenes to improve the narrative arc or character development. In non-fiction, they focus on the clarity and persuasiveness of your arguments.

- **Pacing and Tone:** The editor evaluates the pacing of your manuscript, ensuring it keeps the reader engaged. They also assess the consistency of the tone and voice throughout the book.

Developmental editing is often the most collaborative phase of the editing process, involving significant back-and-forth between the author and editor/writing coach. It's common for a manuscript to undergo substantial revisions during this stage. You could work in a group setting, a Mastermind group, or take a writing class to work through this part of your process. Make sure the group isn't so large that you are unable to get the feedback you need. Find a writing buddy, someone who is also writing a book and who you feel is skilled enough to share in offering support to one another.

If you choose this path, I still suggest you work with good beta readers or have a professional editor review your manuscript before proceeding to the next phase. You can pay an editor to read and offer general thoughts and notes, and if you agree with those suggestions, engage them to do a final developmental pass with you.

Copyediting: Copyediting is the next level of editing and focuses on refining your manuscript at the sentence and paragraph level. It addresses grammar, punctuation, spelling, and syntax, ensuring your writing is clear, consistent, and error-free.

- **Grammar and Punctuation:** The editor corrects any grammatical errors, such as subject-verb agreement, misplaced modifiers, and punctuation mistakes.

- **Consistency**: The editor ensures consistency in spelling, capitalization, and hyphenation, as well as in the use of terms and style throughout the manuscript.

- **Clarity and Flow:** The editor may suggest changes to improve the clarity and flow of your writing. This can involve rephrasing sentences, adjusting paragraph breaks, or clarifying ambiguous statements.

- **Fact-Checking:** Depending on the subject matter, the editor might also check facts, dates, and references for accuracy.

Copyediting is less about making large-scale changes and more about polishing the manuscript to ensure it is professionally presented and easy to read.

Proofreading is the final stage of the editing process. It focuses on catching any remaining typos, formatting issues, and minor errors that were missed in previous rounds of editing.

- **Spelling and Typographical Errors:** The proofreader checks for any spelling mistakes, typographical errors, or missing words.

- **Formatting:** The proofreader ensures that the manuscript adheres to the required formatting guidelines, checking elements such as font consistency, paragraph indentation, line spacing, and page numbering.

- **Final Polish**: This stage is about giving the manuscript one last review to ensure it is as error-free as possible before publication or submission.

Proofreading is typically done after the manuscript has been typeset, making it the last opportunity to catch any issues before the book goes to print or is published.

How to Find and Work with an Editor

Finding the right editor for your manuscript is a critical step in the publishing process. A good editor can elevate your work to new heights, while a poor fit can be frustrating and unproductive. Here's how to find and effectively work with an editor.

Finding an Editor:

- **Research and Recommendations:** Research editors specializing in your genre or subject matter. Personal recommendations from other authors or writing groups can be invaluable. There are also directories and platforms like Reedsy, Editorial Freelancers Association (EFA), and ACES: The Society for Editing, where you can find qualified editors.

- **Evaluate Their Experience**: Look for editors with experience in your genre or area of expertise. Check their portfolios, ask for references, and read testimonials from previous clients. An editor's experience with similar projects can make a significant difference in the quality of feedback you receive.

- **Sample Edits:** Many editors offer sample edits of a few pages to give you a sense of their editing style. This can help you gauge whether their approach aligns with your expectations. A sample edit is also a good way to see how the editor communicates and provides feedback.

Before settling on an editor:

- Have them read a sample of your work.

- Have them review your synopsis and pre-work (i.e., your 5 W's, Outline, etc and get their initial thoughts and feedback. How do they align with your vision?

- Review how they prefer to work/workflow/process – is this workable for you?

- Outline your expectations and have them outline theirs.

- They should provide a scope of work bid outlining everything they will do, a timeline, and costs.

- Have them sign an agreement that includes a work-for-hire agreement.

Here is an example of an agreement you can use for an editor. Please note that I am not a lawyer; this is not legal advice – just an example of what a contract might include. I recommend having a lawyer review any contracts before signing them.

*****

Example of Editorial Services Agreement

This Editorial Services Agreement ("Agreement") is entered into as of [Date] by and between [Author's Full Name] ("Author"), located at [Author's Address], and [Editor's Full Name] ("Editor"), located at [Editor's Address]. The Author and the Editor may collectively be referred to as the "Parties."

1. Scope of Work

The Editor agrees to perform the following services for the Author:

- Developmental Editing

- Copyediting

- Proofreading (Collectively, the "Services")

The Editor shall edit the manuscript titled [Title of Manuscript] ("Manuscript") consisting of approximately [number] words.

2. Compensation

The Author agrees to pay the Editor a total fee of $[Total Amount] for the Services. Payment will be made according to the following schedule:

- **Deposit**: $[Amount] due upon signing this Agreement.

- **First Installment:** $[Amount] due upon delivery of the developmental edit.

- **Second Installment:** $[Amount] due upon delivery of the copyedit.

- **Final Payment:** $[Amount] due upon completion of the proofreading and delivery of the final edited manuscript.

3. Delivery Schedule

The Editor agrees to complete the Services according to the following timeline:

- **Developmental Edit:** Completed by [Date].

- **Copyedit**: Completed by [Date].

- **Proofreading**: Completed by [Date].

The Author will provide the Editor with the Manuscript by [Date]. The Editor agrees to deliver each edited version of the Manuscript to the Author by the agreed-upon deadlines.

4. Revisions

The fee for the Services includes one round of revisions for each stage of editing (developmental, copyediting, and proofreading). Additional revisions beyond the agreed-upon scope will be charged at a rate of $[Hourly Rate] per hour.

5. Confidentiality

The Editor agrees to maintain the confidentiality of the Manuscript and any other materials provided by the Author. The Editor will not disclose any information regarding the Manuscript to any third party without the Author's prior written consent.

6. Work for Hire

The Parties agree that the Manuscript and any edited versions of the Manuscript are being created as a "work for hire" within the meaning of the United States Copyright Act. As such, all rights, title, and interest in the Manuscript, including any copyright, shall belong exclusively to the Author. The Editor hereby waives any and all claims to ownership of the Manuscript or any derivative works thereof.

7. Warranties

The Editor warrants that the Services provided under this Agreement will be original and will not infringe upon the intellectual property rights of any third party. The Editor also warrants that they have the full right and authority to enter into this Agreement and perform the Services.

8. Indemnification

The Author agrees to indemnify and hold harmless the Editor from and against any and all claims, damages, liabilities, and expenses arising out of or related to the Author's use of the Manuscript or any breach of this Agreement by the Author.

9. Termination

Either Party may terminate this Agreement at any time with written notice. If the Agreement is terminated by the Author, the Editor shall be compensated for any Services completed up to the date of termination. If the Editor terminates the Agreement, any portion of the fees paid in advance for Services not yet rendered will be refunded to the Author.

10. Governing Law

This Agreement shall be governed by and construed in accordance with the laws of the State of [State], without regard to its conflict of law principles.

11. Entire Agreement

This Agreement constitutes the entire agreement between the Parties with respect to the subject matter hereof and supersedes all prior or contemporaneous agreements, whether written or oral, relating to such subject matter.

12. Amendments

Any amendments or modifications to this Agreement must be made in writing and signed by both Parties.

13. Signatures

IN WITNESS WHEREOF, the Parties hereto have executed this Agreement as of the date first written above.

[Author's Full Name]

Date: _____

[Editor's Full Name]

Date: _____

Working with an Editor:

- **Set Clear Expectations:** As I said, being upfront about your expectations and having honest and open conversations about the process is key to a successful editing relationship.
- **Be Open to Feedback:** Receiving feedback can be challenging, especially when it involves significant revisions. Remember that the editor's goal is to help you improve

your manuscript. Approach the feedback with an open mind and be willing to make changes that enhance the quality of your work.

- **Communication**: Maintain open and regular communication with your editor throughout the process. If you have questions or concerns about their suggestions, don't hesitate to ask for clarification. Effective communication is key to a successful collaboration.

Revisions and Follow-Up:

- **Revising Based on Feedback:** Once you receive your edited manuscript, take the time to carefully review the editor's comments and suggestions. Consider their advice, but also trust your instincts as the author. It's your story, and you have the final say in how it's presented.

- **Follow-Up Edits:** Depending on the scope of the edits, you may need to go through multiple rounds of revision. Some authors work with their editors through several drafts to refine their manuscripts fully. Make sure to clarify how many rounds of edits are included in your agreement with the editor.

Common Pitfalls to Avoid

Even with a professional editor, there are common pitfalls that writers can encounter during the editing process. Being aware of these can help you navigate the process more smoothly. There is a reason you hired this person to help you.

Resisting Feedback:

- **Taking Criticism:** *DON'T TAKE IT PERSONALLY!* It's natural to feel defensive about your work, especially if you've invested a lot of time and emotion into it. However, it's important to remember that feedback is not a personal attack. Editors are there to help you improve your manuscript, not to tear it down. Try to separate your personal feelings from the feedback process and focus on how the suggestions can enhance your work.

- **Refusing to Make Changes:** BE OPEN TO NEW IDEAS! While it's important to stay true to your vision, refusing to make any changes based on feedback can hinder the development of your manuscript. Listen to constructive criticism and be willing to make revisions where necessary. Often, the changes that are most difficult to accept are the ones that lead to the most significant improvements.

Over-Editing:

- Revising Too Much: It's possible to over-edit your manuscript, especially if you go through many rounds of revisions. Over-editing can lead to a loss of the original voice or spontaneity that made your writing unique. At some point, you need to step back and decide that your manuscript is ready. Trust your instincts and know when it's time to let go.

- Relying Too Heavily on the Editor: While editors provide invaluable feedback, it's important not to rely on them entirely for the success of your manuscript. As the author, you are the final authority on your work. Use the editor's suggestions as a guide, but ensure that the final product reflects your voice and vision.

Skipping Professional Editing:

- **Self-Editing Limitations:** Even the most experienced writers benefit from professional editing. It's easy to miss errors or overlook structural issues in your own work because you're too close to it. Skipping professional editing can result in a manuscript that is less polished and less likely to succeed in the marketplace.

- **Budgeting for Editing:** Professional editing can be expensive, but it's a worthwhile investment in the quality of your book. Skimping on editing to save money can lead to a lower-quality final product, which can affect your book's reception by readers, agents, or publishers. Plan your budget to include professional editing services as a key part of the publishing process. Later in the book, I will outline a suggested budget for self-publishing.

Part 3:
Getting Published

Chapter 8
Choosing Between Self-Publishing and Traditional Publishing

As I've mentioned, you have two main options for getting your book out into the world: self-publishing or working with a traditional publisher. You might have already considered this when you were doing your 5 W's, but if not, here are a few things to think about.

First, let's talk about self-publishing. It costs money—often quite a bit. The saying "you get what you pay for" holds true here. You should be prepared to spend at least $10,000 if not more. This covers everything from editing and design to marketing and distribution.

I understand that not everyone has that kind of money—there are ways to do it for less. Hopefully, reading this book will help. You can find skilled people starting who may not have as much experience in their fields. You can do things yourself or with AI, like writing your social media copy, marketing plan, etc. Be prepared to take the time you need to do it right.

On the other hand, traditional publishing offers its own challenges and rewards. Beyond the big names like Random House, Penguin, and Simon & Schuster, hundreds of smaller boutique publishers might be a better fit for your book. For example, my book The Documentary Filmmaking Masterclass was published by Allworth Press, a publisher that specializes in "how-to" books. It's been in print for five years and still earns royalties—an excellent outcome for that type of book.

You might wonder why they aren't publishing this book. There are a couple of reasons:

1. They don't believe there's a large enough market for books about writing (which I disagree with and why I am really glad I started my own imprint several years ago – more on this in a moment).

2. Working with a traditional publisher means waiting—often 9-12 months or more—before your book even hits the shelves. Publishers have long lead times and need to fit your book into their existing schedule.

Understanding the Realities of Getting a "Book Deal"

One of the most important things to know about publishers is that their primary focus is on sales, which makes sense given the economics of the industry. For new authors, the average sales expectation through a traditional publisher is typically around 2,000 to 5,000 copies—and that's often the publisher's goal just to break even. In reality, most books sell closer to 1,000 to 2,000 copies. The days of large advances and big-budget marketing campaigns are mostly behind us. Today, publishers are looking for a "sure thing."

Of course, they want your book to be good, but what often matters more is the size of your platform. Many publishers won't even consider a book proposal unless the author has a substantial following on social media. They are also increasingly focused on publishing books in the trendiest genres. In an industry where overall book sales are down, and publishers are more risk-averse than ever, they need to be certain they are investing in a product with built-in potential, which begs the question – if I have my own platform, a built-in audience and the ability to market to them, then why do I need a publisher? It's a great question.

The publishing landscape has seen considerable upheaval in recent years, marked by consolidation, layoffs, and shifts in market strategy. Given these dynamics, you might find better opportunities with smaller or mid-sized publishers. However, it's important to be prepared to invest in your own marketing and publicity. Smaller houses often have limited budgets and may not offer any advance; if they do, it is usually quite modest. If you do receive an advance, consider allocating it toward your marketing efforts to maximize your book's exposure.

I'm not trying to dissuade you from working with a publisher. It can still be the best path forward for certain books, providing access to professional editing, design, and distribution channels that can be hard to achieve independently. In my experience, I've had a mix of mediocre and positive outcomes with traditional publishers. Ultimately, I chose to take control of my own publishing journey by creating my own imprint—Rampant Feline Media—to publish my books on my own terms, as well as support authors in writing and publishing their own work.

Another key difference between self-publishing and traditional publishing is ownership. While you should always retain the copyright to your book (if a publisher wants that, it's a red flag), publishers may want to negotiate for other rights, like film adaptations or additional books. It's important to understand what rights they're asking for and what percentage of ownership you'll retain. I'll go into more detail on this in later chapters.

You should also be aware of a type of publisher known as a Vanity Press, which charges you to use their imprint. This is something I offer through my imprint. While this isn't necessarily a bad option, doing your homework is important. Some vanity presses will sell you a package but then try to upsell additional services, which they don't always deliver on. Contact authors who've worked with these companies to get their feedback—what worked well, what didn't, and how the overall pricing and process went.

As with everything, do your research. Ask a lot of questions and trust your instincts. If something sounds too good to be true, it probably is. Working with a publisher—or anyone else you bring onto your team to help get your book out into the world—is like entering a long-term relationship. Watch out for red flags early, be prepared to walk away if necessary, and always aim for open and honest communication about needs, wants, and expectations. This can save you from a lot of headaches, heartbreaks, and legal fees down the line.

Be realistic about your expectations for your book's success. If you think writing the book is the hard part, brace yourself—publishing has its own rollercoaster of highs and lows. I always advise my clients to enter this process with as few expectations as possible. Sure, we all dream of becoming a New York Times bestseller, but most of us won't—and that's okay. You've achieved something that very few people ever will: you've written and published a book, and that alone is worth celebrating.

Remember, my philosophy is simple: if one person reads my book and it brings them joy, offers them hope, or helps them in some way, then it was all worth it.

Chapter 9
Traditional Publishing

Traditional publishing remains one of the most sought-after paths for authors looking to bring their work to a wide audience. While breaking through the barriers is difficult, it's not impossible. Be patient; if your book is well-written, you will most likely find a publisher.

Understanding the Traditional Publishing Process

The traditional publishing process involves multiple stages, each crucial to the success of your book. Understanding these steps can help you navigate the path more effectively.

1. **Querying and Finding an Agent:** The first step in the traditional publishing process is often finding a literary agent. Agents act as intermediaries between authors and publishers, using their industry knowledge and connections to secure publishing deals. Most traditional publishers do not accept unsolicited manuscripts, making an agent essential.

2. **Submission to Publishers:** Once an agent agrees to represent you, they will help you refine your manuscript or book proposal and submit it to publishers. This is often a highly strategic process, where the agent pitches your work to editors at publishing houses that are a good fit for your genre and target audience.

3. **Contract Negotiation:** If a publisher is interested in your work, they will offer you a publishing contract. Your agent will negotiate the terms of this contract on your behalf, ensuring you get the best possible deal. This includes negotiations on advance payments, royalties, rights, and the publication timeline.

4. **Editing and Revision:** Once a contract is signed, the manuscript enters the editing phase. This process involves multiple rounds of editing, including developmental editing, line editing, and copyediting, to polish the manuscript and prepare it for publication.

5. **Production:** After editing, the manuscript moves into production. This includes formatting the book for print and digital formats, designing the cover, and finalizing the layout. At this stage, you may be involved in decisions related to the design and presentation of the book.

6. **Marketing and Publicity:** Publishers typically have marketing and publicity teams that work to promote your book. This includes organizing book tours, setting up interviews, sending out review copies, and managing social media campaigns. While publishers provide support, authors are often expected to actively participate in promoting their work.

7. **Publication and Distribution:** Finally, the book is published and distributed to bookstores, online retailers, and libraries. The success of the book at this stage depends on the effectiveness of the marketing campaign, the distribution network, and word-of-mouth promotion.

How to Find and Approach Literary Agents

Finding the right literary agent is a critical step in the traditional publishing process. Here's how to approach this task:

1. **Research Agents:** Research literary agents representing your genre. Look for agents with a track record of successful book deals, and pay attention to their client lists. Resources like the Association of Authors' Representatives (AAR), QueryTracker, and agency websites are great places to start. If you can, contact some of their clients to understand more about how they work.

2. **Prepare a Query Letter:** A query letter is your first introduction to a literary agent. It should be concise, professional, and tailored to each agent. A standard query letter includes:

    - **Introduction**: Mention why you're approaching this specific agent and briefly introduce your book.

    - **Book Summary:** Provide a compelling synopsis of your book, highlighting the main plot points and what makes it unique.

    - **Author Bio:** Provide a brief bio that includes relevant writing experience, previous publications, and any credentials that establish your authority on the subject matter.

3. **Submission Guidelines:** Each agent has specific submission guidelines, often found on their website. Follow these guidelines carefully, as failing to do so can result in an automatic rejection. This might include submitting a query letter, a synopsis, and the first few chapters of your manuscript.

4. **Be Patient and Persistent:** Many authors will tell you that they received a thousand "no's" before they got a yes; be patient and persistent. Finding an agent can be lengthy, and rejections are common. Revise your query letter and manuscript based on any feedback you receive, and continue submitting until you find the right match.

Crafting a Winning Book Proposal (for Non-Fiction)

For non-fiction books, a well-crafted book proposal is often more important than a completed manuscript. Here's how to create a winning proposal:

1. **Overview**: Begin your proposal with an overview of your book. This should include a brief description of the topic, the book's purpose, and why it is timely or important. The overview sets the stage for the rest of the proposal.

2. **Market Analysis:** Identify your target audience and explain why there is a demand for your book. Include information about market trends, potential competitors, and how your book will stand out in the marketplace.

3. **Author Platform:** In traditional publishing, an author's platform—your ability to reach an audience—is crucial. Detail your existing platform, including your social media following, email list, media appearances, previous publications, and any professional or academic credentials.

4. **Chapter Outline:** Provide a detailed outline of each chapter, including the title and a brief summary. This helps the publisher understand the structure and content of your book.

5. **Sample Chapters:** Include one or two sample chapters to showcase your writing style and the quality of the content. Choose chapters that are representative of the book's tone and subject matter.

6. **Marketing and Promotion Plan:** Publishers want to know how you plan to help promote the book. Outline your marketing and promotion plan, including any connections you have that could be leveraged for publicity, such as media contacts, speaking engagements, or partnerships with organizations.

7. **Competing Titles:** List books that are similar to yours and explain how your book differs or fills a gap in the market. This shows that you have a clear understanding of the market and your book's place within it.

Navigating Contracts and Rights

Publishing contracts can be complex, with many legal and financial implications. Understanding the basics can help you protect your rights and interests.

1. Key Contract Terms:

- **Advance**: The advance is the upfront payment you receive from the publisher. It is an advance against future royalties, meaning you won't receive additional payments until the book earns out this amount.

- **Royalties**: Royalties are payments based on a percentage of book sales. The contract will specify the royalty rates for different formats (hardcover, paperback, eBook, etc.).

- **Rights**: The contract will outline the rights you are granting to the publisher. This includes print rights, digital rights, audio rights, and any subsidiary rights.

- **Manuscript Delivery:** The contract will specify the deadline for submitting your manuscript and any revisions.

- **Publication Timeline:** The contract should include an estimated publication date and any deadlines for the publisher's responsibilities.

- **Reversion of Rights:** This clause specifies the conditions under which rights revert to you, the author, such as if the book goes out of print.

2. Negotiation Tips:

- **Hire an Agent:** A literary agent can negotiate to secure better terms on your behalf.

- **Understand Your Worth:** If you have a strong platform or a unique book, don't be afraid to negotiate for a higher advance or better royalty rates.

- **Retain Key Rights:** Be cautious about giving away too many rights. If you believe certain subsidiary rights, such as film and television rights, could be valuable, consider retaining them.

What Does a Basic Publishing Agreement Look Like?

A basic publishing agreement is a legal contract between the author and the publisher. If you do not have an agent, I recommend having a lawyer work with you on negotiating your contract. I have a rule: I don't negotiate directly with anyone I will eventually be working with creatively. Having someone else be the "bad guy/gal" is best. Remember that everything is negotiable and that while you may be a first-time author, asking for what you want never hurts.

Here are the key components: (Again, I'm not a lawyer, and you should have a lawyer and/or an agent review any agreements- even if you're self-publishing!

1. **Grant of Rights:** The grant of rights clause specifies what rights you are giving to the publisher. This typically includes the right to print, publish, and sell your book in various formats (print, digital, audio) and may include specific territories (e.g., North America, worldwide).

2. **Advances and Royalties:** This section details the financial terms of the contract, including the advance payment and the royalty rates for different formats and territories.

3. **Manuscript Delivery and Acceptance:** This clause outlines the deadlines for delivering the manuscript and any revisions, as well as the criteria for acceptance by the publisher.

4. **Production and Publication:** This section covers the publisher's responsibilities in terms of editing, designing, producing, and marketing the book. It may also include a publication timeline.

5. **Reversion of Rights:** This clause specifies the conditions under which rights revert to the author, such as if the book goes out of print or if sales fall below a certain threshold.

6. **Warranties and Indemnities:** You will be required to warrant that the manuscript is original, does not infringe on any third-party rights, and is not defamatory. The indemnity clause typically requires you to cover the publisher's costs if any legal action arises from your book.

7. **Option Clauses:** Some contracts include an option clause, giving the publisher the first right to publish your next book. These clauses are negotiable, and you should consider the implications carefully.

What are the types of rights publishers are seeking?

Publishers typically seek a wide range of rights to maximize the potential revenue from your book. Here are the most common types of rights:

1. Primary Rights:

- Print Rights: The right to publish and sell your book in physical formats.
- Digital Rights: The right to publish and distribute your book as an eBook.
- Audio Rights: The right to produce and distribute an audiobook version of your book.

2. Subsidiary Rights:

- Translation Rights: The right to translate your book into other languages and sell it in foreign markets.

- Film and Television Rights: The right to adapt your book into a movie, TV show, or other visual media.

- Merchandising Rights: The right to create and sell products based on your book.

- Serial Rights: The right to publish excerpts or serializations of your book in magazines, newspapers, or online platforms.

3. Territorial Rights:

- World Rights: The right to sell your book globally.

- Regional Rights: The right to sell your book in specific regions, such as North America or the United Kingdom.

4. Exclusive vs. Non-Exclusive Rights:

- Exclusive Rights: The publisher has sole rights to the formats and territories granted, meaning you cannot license the same rights to another publisher.

- Non-Exclusive Rights: You retain the ability to license the same rights to multiple parties.

5. Reversion Rights:

These are rights that revert to the author under certain conditions, such as if the book goes out of print or does not meet sales expectations. It's important to negotiate clear terms for reversion rights to ensure that you can regain control of your work if the publisher no longer actively promotes or sells it.

Chapter 10
Working with a Publisher

Navigating the traditional publishing world can be exciting and daunting for authors. This is why it's best to have the support of an expert, either a lawyer or preferably an agent who can negotiate on your behalf. A lawyer might feel like a big expense; however, trust me when I say spend a little upfront to save a lot on the back end. "Legalese" can be confusing, and it doesn't always mean what you think it does. READ EVERY WORD!

The Role of an Editor in Traditional Publishing

When you sign a contract with a traditional publisher, one of your most essential collaborators will be your editor. Editors in traditional publishing houses play a multifaceted role, helping to shape your manuscript into its best possible form and guiding it through the production process. Before you sign your agreement, meet with the editor they have chosen and ensure you are aligned creatively and clearly understand the workflow, etc. Use the same process I outlined above when choosing an editor for your book. You may not have much say in who they choose for you, which may be a sign that this isn't the right publisher for you.

Marketing and Promotion: What to Expect

One of the advantages of working with a traditional publisher is access to their marketing and promotional resources. However, it's important to understand what you can realistically expect regarding marketing support. You will still have to do a lot yourself. Before you sign with a publisher, ask if you can meet with their publicist and/or marketing team; definitely ask them how they intend to market your book, what they will do, their budget, etc., and their expectations of you.

Publisher's Role: Publishers typically handle the broad aspects of marketing and promotion, including:

- **Book Launch**: Coordinating the release date and planning promotional activities around it.

- **Distribution**: Ensuring your book is available in major bookstores, both physical and online.

- **Press Releases and Media Outreach:** Sending out press releases to relevant media outlets and coordinating interviews or appearances.

- **Advance Review Copies (ARCs):** Sending ARCs to reviewers, influencers, and media to generate early buzz.

Author's Role: While publishers do provide support, much of the marketing responsibility still falls on the author. You may need to:

- **Social Media:** Build and maintain an active presence on social media platforms to engage with readers and promote your book.

- **Book Tours and Signings:** Participate in book tours, signings, and other promotional events.

- **Networking**: Leverage your personal and professional networks to spread the word about your book.

- **Content Creation:** Create blog posts, articles, and other content to raise awareness of your book.

Collaboration with Marketing Teams: Work closely with your publisher's marketing team to ensure your promotional efforts align with their strategy. Provide them with insights about your target audience, your platform, and any unique promotional ideas you have.

Understanding Royalties and Advances

Royalties and advances are fundamental aspects of a publishing contract but can also be confusing. Here's a breakdown of what they mean and how they work.

Advances: An advance is an upfront payment you receive from the publisher against future royalties. This means that the publisher is essentially paying you a portion of your expected earnings from book sales in advance.

- How Advances Work: If your advance is $10,000, you won't start receiving royalties until your book has earned that amount in sales. After the advance is "earned out," you'll begin receiving royalty payments.

- **Negotiating Advances:** Advances can vary widely depending on the publisher, the perceived marketability of your book, and your negotiating power. Higher advances are often given to established authors or books expected to sell well.

Royalties: Royalties are the payments you receive based on a percentage of the book's sales. They are typically calculated as a percentage of the book's retail price or the publisher's net receipts.

- **Royalty Rates:** Royalty rates vary but are often in the range of 5-15% for print books, 25-50% for eBooks, and 10-25% for audiobooks.

- **Royalty Statements:** Publishers typically issue royalty statements twice a year, detailing the number of copies sold, the royalties earned, and whether the advance has been earned out.

Earning Out: If your book sells well and earns more than your advance, you start receiving royalty payments. However, if your book does not sell enough copies to cover the advance, you do not have to repay the unearned portion; it's the publisher's risk.

What Does a Basic Publishing Agreement Look Like?

A publishing agreement is a legal contract between you and the publisher outlining the terms under which your book will be published. Here are the key elements you'll find in a typical publishing agreement:

Grant of Rights: This section specifies the rights you are granting to the publisher, such as the right to publish the book in certain formats (print, digital, audio) and in certain territories (worldwide, North America, etc.).

Advance and Royalties: The agreement will detail the amount of the advance, how it will be paid, and the royalty rates for different formats and territories.

Manuscript Delivery: This clause specifies the deadline for delivering the completed manuscript and any revisions.

Publication and Marketing: The publisher's responsibilities in terms of editing, designing, publishing, and marketing the book are outlined here, including timelines for publication.

Subsidiary Rights: This section outlines any additional rights being granted to the publisher, such as translation rights, film and television rights, and merchandising rights.

Termination and Reversion of Rights: This clause explains the conditions under which the contract can be terminated and how rights revert to the author if the book goes out of print or fails to meet certain sales thresholds.

Warranties and Indemnities: You'll be required to warrant that your manuscript is original, does not infringe on any third-party rights, and is not defamatory. The indemnity clause typically requires you to cover the publisher's costs if any legal action arises from your book.

Option Clauses: Some contracts include an option clause, giving the publisher the first right to publish your next book. These clauses can be negotiable.

It's crucial to have an agent or an attorney with experience in publishing contracts review any agreement before you sign it. Publishing agreements are complex, and understanding the terms is essential to protecting your rights as an author.

What Are the Types of Rights Publishers Seek?

Publishers typically seek a variety of rights to maximize their ability to generate revenue from your book. Here's a closer look at the types of rights that publishers might want:

Primary Rights:

- **Print Rights:** The right to publish and sell your book in physical formats, including hardcover and paperback.

- **Digital Rights**: The right to publish and distribute your book as an eBook.

- **Audio Rights**: The right to produce and distribute an audiobook version of your book.

Subsidiary Rights:

- **Translation Rights:** The right to translate your book into other languages and sell it in foreign markets.

- **Film and Television Rights:** The right to adapt your book into a movie, TV show, or other visual media.

- **Merchandising Rights**: The right to create and sell products based on your book, such as apparel, toys, or posters.

- **Serial Rights:** The right to publish excerpts or serializations of your book in magazines, newspapers, or online platforms, either before (first serial) or after (second serial) publication.

Territorial Rights:

- **World Rights:** The right to sell your book globally.

- **Regional Rights:** The right to sell your book in specific regions, such as North America, the United Kingdom, or specific countries.

Exclusive vs. Non-Exclusive Rights:

- **Exclusive Rights:** The publisher has sole rights to the formats and territories granted, meaning you cannot license the same rights to another publisher.

- **Non-Exclusive Rights:** You retain the ability to license the same rights to multiple parties.

Moral Rights and Adaptation Rights: Some contracts may seek to limit or obtain waivers for moral rights (e.g., the right to object to derogatory treatment of your work) and may also include adaptation rights for creating derivative works, such as graphic novels or stage plays.

Reversion Rights: These are rights that revert to the author under certain conditions, such as if the book goes out of print or does not meet sales expectations. It's important to negotiate clear terms for reversion rights to ensure that you can regain control of your work if the publisher no longer actively promotes or sells it.

Right of First Refusal: Some contracts include a right of first refusal or an option clause, where the publisher has the right to review and potentially publish your next work before you offer it to other publishers.

Understanding the types of rights publishers seek and how they can affect your book's future is crucial when entering a publishing agreement. Retaining some rights can allow you to pursue additional opportunities or maintain control over how your work is used.

Part 4:
Self-Publishing: The Truth about Self-Publishing

I believe self-publishing has gotten an unfair reputation over the years. Sure, in any industry where people decide to go "rogue" and do things their own way, there will always be those who criticize. Some publishers, and even authors who've gone the traditional route, love to play the shame game and act as if self-publishing is somehow less legitimate. Well, I'm here to tell you—that's nonsense. Today, self-publishing can be the best choice for your book, depending on your goals, audience, and timeline.

That said, self-publishing doesn't mean you have to go it alone—and, frankly, you shouldn't. If you followed the 5 W's at the beginning of your process, you already know a lot about your audience: who they are, what they want, where to find them, and how to speak to them. This knowledge is gold, and now it's time to put it to work with a smart, strategic marketing plan.

Developing Your Marketing Strategy

Creating an effective marketing plan is crucial, but it doesn't have to break the bank. The key is to start early and do your homework. There are plenty of marketing companies and social media "gurus" out there who will promise you the moon and charge you a small fortune for it. Be cautious of these folks. You don't need to spend a ton of money to reach your audience if you've done your research and crafted a targeted strategy.

Begin thinking about your marketing plan while you're still writing your book. Explore all your options and consider what will work best for reaching your particular audience. Will they respond to social media campaigns, email newsletters, podcasts, or live events? What platforms do they spend their time on? What kind of content do they engage with most?

I always advise my clients to put as much energy into planning how they'll market their book as they do into writing it. Remember, your marketing starts the minute you start writing. Every decision you make—whether it's about the title, the cover, or the tone—should be made with your target audience in mind.

I want to give a shout-out to one of my favorite Book Marketing gurus, Mary Adams. Together, we have created multiple best-selling releases. Later, I will share how to find and work with the right people to support your book.

To answer everyone's burning question, yes, you can use AI to create a marketing plan, social posts, etc. It's not a bad start. But it is by no means definitive, nor is it the panacea many people pretend it is.

AI requires specific prompts to produce the compelling and specific posts you need. I'm not going to lie; I sometimes insert my synopsis into Chat and ask it to write out a plan; however, I go over every word and every hashtag and refine it, clarify it, and make darn sure it is truly representative of my work and the message I want to convey.

As I said, it's a starting point, not the end of your work. As I stated earlier in this book, don't get hypnotized by your finished manuscript; the same goes for AI. Do not get lulled into a false sense of "oooh, this was so easy" and hit send without doing a solid review and edit.

Marketing Begins Early

If you've chosen to self-publish, understand that your marketing efforts begin from day one. As soon as you start writing, you should think about how you will reach your audience. This means building a presence, creating buzz, and establishing yourself as someone worth listening to.

Start building your email list as early as possible. Offer something of value—like a sample chapter, an exclusive article, or a behind-the-scenes look at your writing process—in exchange for email sign-ups. Engage with potential readers on social media by sharing insights, asking questions, and creating conversations around your topic or genre.

Think of yourself not just as an author but as a brand. Your brand is how you present yourself and your book to the world. It's the promise of what readers can expect when they pick up your book. So, consider what makes you unique and how you can communicate that through everything you do—from your social media posts to your email signature.

Be Smart About Your Resources

You don't need to spend a fortune to market your book effectively. There are countless free or low-cost ways to promote your book if you're willing to be creative and put in the effort. Start with what you have: your network. Reach out to friends, family, colleagues, and anyone else who might be interested in your book. Don't be afraid to ask them to help spread the word.

Leverage social media, but do it wisely. Find out where your audience spends their time—whether it's Instagram, TikTok, LinkedIn, or somewhere else—and focus your efforts there. Share content that's relevant to your book, your brand, and your audience's interests. Use visuals, videos, and storytelling to grab attention and keep it.

Consider guest blogging or writing articles for sites that your target audience frequents. Look for podcasts that align with your book's theme or audience and pitch yourself as a guest. Collaborate with other authors or influencers in your niche to cross-promote each other's work. Think beyond the traditional book launch—maybe a virtual event, a series of webinars, or even an interactive book club could be a better fit for your audience.

Keep It Real

Most importantly, keep it real. Be genuine in your marketing efforts. Readers can sense when someone is being authentic versus when they're just trying to make a sale. Share your journey, your struggles, your breakthroughs. Let your personality come through. People are more likely to support an author they know and trust.

Remember, marketing isn't just about selling books—it's about building relationships and creating a community of readers who are excited about what you have to offer. It's about making sure that when your book does come out, there's already a group of people who are eager to buy it, read it, and talk about it.

Don't Wait—Start Now

If you've decided to self-publish, don't wait until your book is finished to start thinking about marketing. The earlier you start, the more time you have to build momentum and connect with your audience. Make a plan, get creative, and start now.

Start building your platform and creating social media pages, either as an author or for your book. I prefer to have an author page—that way, I can promote all my books. But if you're a one-and-done writer, then have it focus on the book. Start a Substack or other blogging page (I'll explain these later). The point is to begin to build a relationship with your audience so that come launch day, they are chomping at the keyboard to buy your book!

Self-publishing doesn't mean you're going it alone; it means you're in the driver's seat, with full control over your book and its journey to the readers who need it. So embrace that power, be smart about your strategy, and put in the work to make sure your book gets the attention it deserves.

As you embark on your self-publishing journey, it's essential to start building your author platform even before your book is finished. Establishing a presence early on will help you connect with your target audience and increase your chances of selling books once your work is published. Social Media can be daunting, and while it's key to your success, it isn't the only way to sell books.

One effective way to begin is by joining online communities that align with your genre. Look for Facebook groups, subreddits, and other forums where readers and writers in your niche gather. Look for book clubs and groups that align with your theme/genre and join them! Get out and kiss some babies and shake some hands! Engaging in these spaces will help you learn from others, gain visibility, and even find beta readers who can provide valuable feedback on your manuscript.

Consider starting a blog on platforms like Substack, Patreon, or Medium, which enable you to share your thoughts, ideas, and excerpts from your book while growing a dedicated following. Building your platform early on helps you cultivate an audience and generate interest in your book long before it's published. In the following chapters, I will dive deeper into these platforms, but here's a quick pro tip: Don't simply "blog your book." Instead, write about topics related to your book and use the content that didn't make it into the final draft—those great ideas that still have value. These pieces can serve as powerful promotional tools to attract and engage potential readers.

Chapter 11
The Self-Publishing Revolution

Self-publishing has transformed the book industry, offering authors unprecedented opportunities. With the advent of digital platforms, print-on-demand technology, and global distribution channels, authors now have the power to publish their work independently and reach readers around the world.

Pros and Cons of Self-Publishing

Self-publishing offers numerous advantages, but it also comes with its own set of challenges. Understanding both sides can help you make an informed decision about whether self-publishing is the right path for you.

Pros of Self-Publishing:

- **Creative Control:** As a self-published author, you retain full creative control over your work. You make all the decisions, from the content and cover design to pricing and marketing strategies. This autonomy allows you to bring your vision to life without the constraints of traditional publishing.

- **Higher Royalties:** Self-publishing platforms typically offer higher royalty rates compared to traditional publishing. Depending on the platform and pricing model, you can earn between 35% and 70% of the sales price, significantly more than traditional publishers' standard 5% to 15% royalties.

- **Speed to Market**: Traditional publishing can be a lengthy process, often taking years from manuscript submission to publication. In contrast, self-publishing allows you to get your book to market quickly, sometimes in just a matter of weeks.

- **Ownership of Rights:** When you self-publish, you retain all rights to your book, including print, digital, and subsidiary rights. This means you have the freedom to explore other revenue streams, such as foreign translations, audiobooks, or film adaptations.

- **Global Reach:** Self-publishing platforms like Amazon Kindle Direct Publishing (KDP), Apple Books, Ingram Spark, and others offer global distribution, allowing your book to reach readers around the world without the need for a traditional publisher's network.

Cons of Self-Publishing:

- **Upfront Costs:** Unlike traditional publishing, where the publisher bears the cost of production, marketing, and distribution, self-publishing requires you to invest your own money. This can include expenses for professional editing, cover design, formatting, and marketing.

- **Limited Marketing and Distribution Support:** In self-publishing, you are responsible for marketing your book. While platforms may provide some tools and resources, the burden of promotion largely falls on the author. Without the backing of a traditional publisher's marketing team, gaining visibility can be challenging.

- **Time and Effort:** Self-publishing demands a significant amount of time and effort. In addition to writing, you'll need to manage all aspects of the publishing process, from production to sales and marketing. This can be overwhelming, especially for first-time authors.

- **Perception and Stigma:** Although the stigma surrounding self-publishing has diminished in recent years, some readers, reviewers, and bookstores still view traditionally published books as more legitimate. This perception can impact your ability to secure physical store reviews, awards, and shelf space.

- **Quality Control:** In self-publishing, the quality of your book is entirely your responsibility. Without the support of a traditional publisher's editorial team, you must ensure that your book is professionally edited, formatted, and designed to meet industry standards.

Choosing the Right Platform

Selecting the right self-publishing platform is a crucial step in your publishing journey. Different platforms offer various services, distribution options, and royalty structures. Here's an overview of some of the most popular platforms and factors to consider when making your choice. Some people choose to use multiple platforms, like KDP and IngramSpark. Be sure to follow all the guidelines and steps on all platforms you choose when combining distribution.

1. **Amazon Kindle Direct Publishing (KDP):**

    - **Overview**: KDP is the most popular self-publishing platform, offering both ebook and print-on-demand services. It provides access to Amazon's vast global customer base, making it a powerful tool for reaching readers.

    - **Pros**: Easy to use, global reach, high royalties (70% on ebooks priced between $2.99 and $9.99), options for Kindle Unlimited and Kindle Select (exclusive distribution programs).

    - **Cons**: Amazon's exclusivity requirements for Kindle Select can limit your ability to distribute your ebook on other platforms. KDP's market dominance means you may face stiff competition.

2. **Apple Books:**

    - **Overview**: Apple Books offers a strong platform for self-publishing ebooks, particularly for authors looking to reach readers who use Apple devices.

    - **Pros**: High royalties (up to 70%), no exclusivity requirements, access to a large global audience of Apple users, integration with iBooks Author for enhanced ebooks.

    - **Cons**: It has a lower market share compared to Amazon and is limited to Apple's ecosystem, which may exclude non-Apple users.

3. **Barnes & Noble Press:**

    - **Overview**: Barnes & Noble Press is the self-publishing platform for ebooks and print books from the largest brick-and-mortar bookstore chain in the U.S.

    - **Pros**: Potential for in-store placement in Barnes & Noble stores, high royalties (up to 65%), no exclusivity requirements, access to Nook readers.

    - **Cons**: Smaller market share compared to Amazon, primarily U.S.-focused audience.

4. **IngramSpark:**

    - **Overview**: IngramSpark offers both ebook and print-on-demand services. Its extensive distribution options through the Ingram Book Group reach bookstores, libraries, and online retailers worldwide.

    - **Pros**: Wide distribution network, high-quality print-on-demand services, access to bookstores and libraries, professional-level tools.

    - **Cons**: Upfront costs for setup and distribution, more complex interface, lower royalties on some sales channels.

**This is my chosen platform. People have opinions about each of these options. Personally, I have found that Ingram Spark offers me the most value and worldwide distribution.

5. Kobo Writing Life:

- **Overview**: Kobo Writing Life is a self-publishing platform with a strong international presence, especially in Canada and Europe.

- **Pros**: High royalties (up to 70%), no exclusivity requirements, global distribution, integration with OverDrive for library distribution.

- **Cons**: Smaller market share compared to Amazon, primarily focused on digital distribution (no print-on-demand).

Factors to Consider When Choosing a Platform:

- **Distribution Reach:** Consider where you want your book to be available. Platforms like KDP, IngramSpark, and Kobo offer extensive distribution options if global reach is important.

- **Royalties and Pricing:** Evaluate each platform's royalty rates and pricing flexibility. Some platforms offer higher royalties but may have restrictions on pricing or exclusivity.

- **Ease of Use:** Some platforms are more user-friendly than others. If you're new to self-publishing, you might prioritize a platform that is easy to navigate and provides robust customer support.

- **Print vs. Digital Focus:** Determine whether you need print-on-demand services in addition to digital distribution. Platforms like IngramSpark and KDP offer both, while others focus solely on ebooks.

Ebooks vs. Print: Formats and Considerations

Deciding whether to publish your book as an ebook, print book, or both is a critical decision in the self-publishing process. Each format has its own advantages and challenges.

Ebooks:

- **Pros**:

  o Lower Production Costs: Ebooks are generally less expensive to produce since there are no printing or shipping costs.

  o Instant Delivery: Readers can instantly purchase and download your book, leading to immediate gratification and potentially higher sales.

- o Global Distribution: Ebooks can be sold and delivered to readers worldwide, expanding your reach.
- o Flexible Pricing: Ebooks allow for more flexible pricing strategies, including promotions, discounts, and bundling with other digital products.
- Cons:
- o Digital Exclusivity: Some readers still prefer physical books, so limiting your publication to an ebook might exclude part of your potential audience.
- o Market Saturation: The ebook market is highly competitive, with millions of titles available. Standing out can be challenging.
- o Piracy: Ebooks are more susceptible to piracy, as digital files can be easily copied and shared illegally.

Print Books:
- **Pros**:
- o Tangible Product: Many readers prefer the feel of a physical book. Print books can also be more impressive as gifts or collectibles.
- o Bookstore Presence: Print books can be sold in bookstores and libraries, providing an additional sales channel and visibility.
- o Signings and Events: Print books allow for author signings, which can be a powerful marketing tool and a way to connect with readers in person.
- **Cons**:
- o Higher Production Costs: Printing, shipping, and inventory management involve significant upfront costs.
- o Distribution Challenges: Getting your print book into physical bookstores requires navigating complex and competitive distribution networks.
- o Longer Time to Market: Print books typically take longer to produce and distribute compared to ebooks.

Combination Approach:

This is my preferred option. You can sell off of multiple sites, as well as directly from your own website or platform.

- Many self-published authors publish both ebook and print formats to maximize their reach and sales potential. This approach allows you to cater to both digital and traditional readers, providing multiple revenue streams.

- When publishing both formats, ensure that your pricing strategy makes sense across different channels. For example, ebook prices are typically lower than print prices, but they should still reflect the value of your work.

Whatever platform you choose, make sure to read the fine print! Using a third party requires careful attention to detail. I recommend setting up a separate bank account to manage your earnings and keep track of your sales. Additionally, be sure to request regular reports from the service printing your book to stay informed about your progress.

Monitoring Sales

As an independent self-published author, tracking your sales is crucial to understanding your book's performance and optimizing your marketing efforts. Here are several ways to effectively track your sales:

1. Use the Reporting Tools of Each Platform

Most self-publishing platforms provide built-in reporting tools to help you track your sales. Here are a few examples:

- **Amazon Kindle Direct Publishing (KDP):** Offers a detailed dashboard that tracks book sales, Kindle Unlimited page reads, and royalties in real-time. You can generate reports for specific timeframes and analyze data by title, marketplace, and format.

- **Barnes & Noble Press:** Provides sales reports that show your earnings and units sold. You can filter reports by date, book, and format.

- **Apple Books for Authors:** Features a sales and trends tool where you can monitor your daily, weekly, or monthly sales and download reports in various formats.

- **IngramSpark:** Allows you to access sales reports that provide detailed information on the number of books sold, where they were sold, and your royalties.

2. Consolidate Sales Data with Aggregators

If you publish on multiple platforms, consider using an aggregator like Draft2Digital or Smashwords. These services distribute your book to various retailers and provide a centralized dashboard for tracking sales across multiple outlets. Aggregators can save you time by compiling all your sales data in one place.

3. Set Up Google Analytics for Your Author's Website

If you have a website or blog, use Google Analytics to monitor traffic, user behavior, and referral sources. You can set up specific goals, such as tracking clicks on buy links or visits to your book's landing page, to gauge how well your promotional efforts are driving sales.

4. Use Affiliate Links to Track Sales

Consider signing up for affiliate programs with platforms like Amazon, where you can generate unique affiliate links for your book. This allows you to earn additional income while also gaining insights into how many people purchase your book through these links. The data from affiliate sales can help you identify which marketing efforts are most effective.

5. Monitor Print-on-Demand Sales with Regular Reports

If you use print-on-demand services (like Amazon KDP Print or IngramSpark), make sure to regularly check their sales reports. Set a schedule to download and review these reports—daily, weekly, or monthly—to stay on top of your print book sales.

6. Use Book Sales Tracking Tools

Consider using specialized book sales tracking tools, such as:

- **BookReport**: An extension that integrates with your KDP dashboard, providing more detailed, visually appealing sales analytics.

- **TrackerBox**: A desktop application that consolidates sales data from multiple retailers into one easy-to-read report.

- **Kindlepreneur's Book Profit Calculator:** Helps estimate royalties and track potential earnings based on your book's price, platform, and royalties percentage.

7. Ask for Regular Reports from Your Print and Distribution Partners

If you're working with a print or distribution partner, request regular sales reports. Make sure they provide detailed data, including the number of copies sold, locations, and any returns or refunds.

8. Track Sales Manually

While more time-consuming, you can also track sales manually using a spreadsheet. Create a template where you input data from each platform regularly. Include columns for the platform, date, units sold, revenue earned, and any associated costs to calculate net profit. This method can provide a comprehensive overview of your total sales across all channels.

9. Leverage Social Media and Direct Sales Data

If you sell books directly through social media, email lists, or at events, keep meticulous records of these transactions. Use simple tools like spreadsheets or software like QuickBooks or Wave to record sales, customer details, and any promotional offers used.

By combining these strategies, you can gain a comprehensive understanding of your book's performance, identify trends, and make data-driven decisions to improve your marketing and sales efforts.

Chapter 12
Preparing for Self-Publishing

ISBNs, Barcodes

Self-publishing involves much more than simply uploading your manuscript to a platform. Careful preparation is essential to ensure your book is competitive and professional.

The first thing you will need is an ISBN.
What is an ISBN, and Why Do You Need One?

ISBN stands for International Standard Book Number. It is a unique identifier assigned to each edition and format of a book, which allows it to be recognized and tracked in bookstores, libraries, online retailers, and distribution systems worldwide.

Why You Need an ISBN:

- **Identification**: An ISBN uniquely identifies your book and its specific format (e.g., hardcover, paperback, ebook) and distinguishes it from other books on the market.

- **Distribution**: Many retailers, distributors, and libraries require an ISBN to carry your book. Without an ISBN, your book may not be listed in important sales and distribution databases.

- **Sales Tracking:** ISBNs are used in sales tracking systems to report and monitor book sales, which is important for both you as the author and any distribution partners.

- **Credibility**: Having an ISBN gives your book a professional appearance, indicating that it is a legitimate, published work. It can also enhance your credibility as an author.

How to Get an ISBN

1. Purchasing an ISBN:

- **In the United States,** ISBNs are issued by Bowker (through their MyIdentifiers.com service). You can purchase a single ISBN or a block of ISBNs if you plan to publish multiple books or editions.

    o   Cost: A single ISBN costs around $125, but you can purchase blocks of 10, 100, or more at a reduced cost per ISBN.

- **In Other Countries:** ISBNs are issued by designated agencies in different countries. For example, in the UK, ISBNs are issued by Nielsen, and in Canada, ISBNs are free and can be obtained through the Canadian ISBN Agency.

- **Self-Publishing Platforms:** Some self-publishing platforms, such as Amazon Kindle Direct Publishing (KDP) or IngramSpark, offer free ISBNs as part of their services. However, these ISBNs often list the platform as the publisher rather than you or your imprint, which might limit your control over distribution.

2. Assigning ISBNs:

- **Each Format Requires a Separate ISBN:** You need a different ISBN for each format of your book (e.g., one for the paperback, another for the hardcover, and another for the ebook). This allows each version to be identified and sold separately.

- **ISBN for Different Editions:** If you publish a new edition of your book (such as a second edition with significant changes), you'll need a new ISBN for that edition.

Do You Need a Barcode?

What is a Barcode?

- A barcode is a graphical representation of your book's ISBN in a format that retailers can scan at the point of sale. It typically includes the ISBN and additional pricing information.

Why You Need a Barcode:

- **Retail Sales:** Most physical bookstores and retailers require a barcode to sell your book. The barcode is used at checkout to scan the ISBN and manage inventory.

- **Inventory Management:** Barcodes facilitate inventory tracking, making it easier for retailers and distributors to manage and reorder your book.

How to Get a Barcode:

- **Through ISBN Agencies**: Many ISBN agencies offer the option to purchase a barcode when you buy your ISBN. For example, Bowker allows you to buy a barcode along with your ISBN.

- **Self-Publishing Platforms:** Some self-publishing platforms generate barcodes for you when you upload your book's cover, especially if they issue your ISBN. This service might be free or included in the cost of the ISBN.

- **Online Barcode Generators:** You can also use online services to generate a barcode from your ISBN. These services often allow you to download the barcode in different formats, which you can then add to your book's cover design.

Summary: Do You Need an ISBN and Barcode?

- **Print Books:** You need an ISBN for each print book format (e.g., hardcover, paperback). You also need a barcode if you plan to sell your book in physical bookstores or through distributors.

- **Ebooks**: You need a separate ISBN for your ebook, though some platforms like Amazon KDP assign an ASIN (Amazon Standard Identification Number) instead of requiring an ISBN. However, you should have an ISBN if you plan to distribute your ebook outside of Amazon, such as through Apple Books or Kobo.

- **Barcodes**: A barcode is necessary for any print edition of your book that you plan to sell through physical retailers. It ensures that your book can be scanned and sold in stores.

Cover and Interior Design

Designing a Professional Book Cover

The cover of your book is a critical factor in its success, serving as the first impression for potential readers and significantly impacting their decision to purchase. In today's digital marketplace, where your book is often viewed as a small thumbnail, your cover design must be both eye-catching and legible at reduced sizes. This means focusing on bold, clear typography, striking visuals, and a layout that stands out on any screen. To ensure your cover is noticed in a sea of tiny images, take the time to study successful covers in your genre and analyze what makes them pop. Consider how your cover can differentiate itself through unique color schemes, memorable imagery, or an unconventional design approach that captures the essence of your book while grabbing attention among countless other options.

1. **Importance of a Professional Cover:** Your book cover is a visual representation of your work, and it should convey the genre, tone, and quality of the content within. A professional cover can:

- **Grab Attention**: A striking cover design can draw the eye of potential readers browsing online or in stores.

- **Communicate Genre:** The cover should instantly communicate the genre of your book, whether it's a mystery, romance, science fiction, or non-fiction.

- **Build Credibility:** A professional cover enhances your credibility as an author and signals to readers that the book is of high quality.

2. **Hiring a Professional Designer**: Unless you have a strong graphic design background, hiring a professional cover designer is advisable. Although I sometimes use AI to get ideas, I do not recommend using AI to design your cover. You will most likely get a design that has been copied (although altered) that isn't unique.

   Portfolio Review: Look for designers with a portfolio that aligns with your book's genre and style. Many designers specialize in specific genres, which can be an advantage.

   - **Experience and Reviews:** Check for expertise in the publishing industry and read reviews or testimonials from other authors who have worked with the designer.

   - **Collaboration**: A good designer will work collaboratively with you, listening to your ideas and incorporating your feedback into the final design.

3. **Key Elements of a Book Cover**: A successful book cover typically includes the following elements:

   - **Title and Author Name:** These should be prominently displayed and easily read, even at thumbnail size.

   - **Imagery**: Choose imagery that reflects the content and mood of your book. Avoid overly complex or cluttered designs.

   - **Typography**: The font choice is critical. It should be legible and appropriate for your genre. For example, a horror novel might use a bold, edgy font, while a romance might favor a softer, more elegant typeface.

   - **Color Scheme**: The colors you choose can evoke certain emotions and help establish the book's tone. Bright, bold colors might be suitable for a high-energy thriller, while muted tones might be better for literary fiction.

Ok, you have the front cover… what about the back?

To create a compelling back cover for your book, you should focus on elements that capture attention and entice readers to dive into your story. Here's what to include:

1. A Captivating Book Blurb

The blurb is the most crucial element on the back cover. It should be a concise, engaging summary that highlights your book's central conflict or theme without revealing too much. Aim for a few short paragraphs that set the tone, introduce key characters or concepts, and create a sense of intrigue or urgency. Use powerful, evocative language to hook the reader and leave them wanting more.

2. Author Bio

Include a brief author bio that establishes your credibility and connection to the book's subject or genre. Mention any relevant accomplishments, previous works, or unique experiences that make you an authority or interesting voice in your field. Keep it personable and relatable to build a connection with your potential readers.

3. Endorsements or Testimonials

Add a few endorsements or testimonials if you have them. Quotes from reputable sources—such as other authors, industry professionals, or reviewers—can provide social proof and add credibility to your book. Choose endorsements that are specific and highlight what makes your book unique or compelling.

4. Compelling Tagline or Hook

Consider including a catchy tagline or a single sentence that captures the essence of your book. This can be positioned above the blurb or at the top of the cover. A strong, memorable hook instantly draws readers in and makes your book stand out.

5. Genre Indicators and Keywords

Subtly include genre indicators or keywords that help readers immediately identify what kind of book they're looking at. For example, if it's a thriller, you might mention "A Gripping Psychological Thriller" in the description. This helps target the right audience and ensures readers know they are in the right place.

6. Professional Design Elements

Ensure that the back cover's design is consistent with your book's front cover and overall theme. Use matching fonts, colors, and layout styles to create a cohesive look. Include your publisher's logo, imprint name, and the ISBN and barcode at the bottom.

7. Call to Action

While not always necessary, a subtle call to action can be effective. Encourage the reader to start reading now or mention a special offer for signing up for a newsletter or following on social media. Keep this part brief and non-intrusive.

By strategically combining these elements, your back cover will be an enticing marketing tool that piques curiosity and persuades readers to choose your book over others.

How do you organize a book?

A well-organized book layout not only enhances the reader's experience but also conveys professionalism and clarity. Here is a general structure for a book, detailing the key sections in the order they typically appear:

1. Half-Title Page

- The half-title page, also known as the "bastard title," contains only the book title, often in a simplified or minimalistic design. It is the very first page a reader sees upon opening the book and sets a clean and focused tone.

2. Blank or Optional Copyright Page

- After the half-title, there may be a blank page or a page for optional content like quotes or a dedication.

3. Title Page

- The title page includes the book's full title, the subtitle (if applicable), the author's name, and the publisher's name and logo. This page is usually more stylized and acts as an official declaration of the book's identity.

4. Copyright Page

- The copyright page typically appears on the back of the title page. It includes copyright information, publication date, edition details, ISBN, publisher information, disclaimers, and any credits for design, editing, or illustrations. If the book is dedicated to someone, this page might also include a short dedication note.

Here's an example:

Copyright © 2024 by Jane Doe

All rights reserved.

No part of this book may be reproduced, distributed, or transmitted in any form or by any means, including photocopying, recording, or other electronic or mechanical methods, without the prior written permission of the publisher, except in the case of brief quotations in critical reviews and certain other noncommercial uses permitted by copyright law.

Published by Doe Publishing

123 Main Street
New York, NY 10001
www.doepublishing.com
ISBN: 978-1-23456-789-0
Cover design by John Smith
Interior design by Jane Lee
Printed in the United States of America
First Edition: 2024

5. Dedication Page (Optional)

- This page is where the author dedicates the book to someone special. It's a simple, single page with a brief, personal message or dedication.

6. Epigraph (Optional)

- An epigraph is a short quotation or excerpt that sets the tone or theme of the book. It is placed on its own page, often before the main content starts.

7. Table of Contents

- The table of contents (TOC) lists all the major sections, chapters, or parts of the book, along with their corresponding page numbers. This section helps readers navigate the book and quickly locate specific content.

8. Foreword (Optional best for Non-Fiction)

- The foreword is usually written by someone other than the author, such as a notable figure in the field, and provides an endorsement or a personal perspective on the book's subject matter.

9. Preface (Optional best for Non-Fiction)

- The preface is written by the author and offers insight into why they wrote the book, their inspiration, or any acknowledgments. It often includes background information or context that helps the reader understand the book's purpose.

10. Acknowledgments (Optional)

- The acknowledgments page is where the author thanks individuals, organizations, or entities that contributed to the creation of the book. This can appear at the beginning or end of the book, depending on the author's preference.

11. Introduction (Optional best for Non-Fiction)

- The introduction provides an overview of the book's main themes, objectives, and structure. It's designed to prepare the reader for what's to come and establish a connection between the author and the reader.

12. Main Content

- This is the core of the book and consists of chapters or sections. Each chapter typically starts on a new page and may have its own title, heading, or number. Content should be organized logically and consistently, following the structure outlined in the table of contents.

13. Conclusion or Final Chapter

- The conclusion or final chapter wraps up the main ideas, themes, or arguments presented in the book. It provides closure and may include a call to action, final thoughts, or a summary.

14. Appendices (Optional)

- Appendices provide additional information that supports the main content but is too detailed or tangential to be included in the main chapters. Examples include data tables, charts, supplemental texts, or extended references.

15. Endnotes or Footnotes (Optional)

- If the book includes citations, references, or additional notes that don't fit within the main text, these can be compiled as endnotes at the end of the book or as footnotes at the bottom of individual pages.

16. Bibliography or References (Optional)

- A bibliography or reference section lists all the sources cited throughout the book. This is particularly important for non-fiction books, academic works, or research-based content.

17. Glossary (Optional)

- A glossary provides definitions or explanations for specialized terms, jargon, or concepts used throughout the book. It's helpful for readers who may be unfamiliar with certain terminology.

18. Index (Optional)

- The index is an alphabetical list of names, places, subjects, keywords found in the book, and page numbers where they appear. This is particularly useful for non-fiction books to help readers quickly locate specific information.

19. About the Author

- This section provides a brief biography of the author, including their background, achievements, previous works, and any relevant credentials. It may also include a photo of the author and contact information, such as their website or social media profiles.

20. Back Matter (Optional)

- Back matter may include additional materials like a preview of the author's next book, a reader's guide, a list of other works by the author, or any bonus content such as interviews, Q&A, or discussion questions.

21. Blank Pages or Endpapers

- To maintain the aesthetics of the book's design, there may be a few blank pages or decorative endpapers at the very end of the book. These help create a professional look and balance the book's layout.

Ok- you might be overwhelmed. There are people who can help you:

There are several platforms where you can hire a professional designer to create a high-quality cover and interior design for your book. These platforms offer a range of services, from freelance marketplaces to specialized book design services.

Here are some of the top platforms to consider:

When I'm looking for a new designer, I use Fiverr, although many of these platforms have wonderful creatives who will work within your budget.

You will need a cover and interior design for both your E-Book and print. Each requires a different format. You will get the specs from your chosen printer, and you should hire a designer who has worked with that printer a couple of times to make sure your delivery and QC (Quality control) go smoothly.

1. **Reedsy**

    - **Overview**: Reedsy is a marketplace specifically designed for authors. It connects you with professional editors, designers, and marketers with experience in the publishing industry.

    - **Features**:

        o   Access to vetted professionals with experience in book design.

        o   Ability to review portfolios and read testimonials from other authors.

        o   Direct communication with designers for a collaborative process.

    - Best For Authors looking for highly qualified, industry-specific designers who understand the nuances of book design.

2. **99designs**

    - **Overview**: 99designs is a popular platform for sourcing creative professionals, including book cover designers. It allows you to run a design contest where multiple designers submit concepts, or you can hire a designer directly.

    - **Features**:

        o Design contests where you receive multiple design concepts from different designers.

        o The option to work one-on-one with a designer of your choice.

        o Comprehensive portfolios to review before hiring.

    - Best For: Authors who want to see a variety of design ideas before selecting the final cover or who prefer the flexibility of choosing from multiple options.

3. **Fiverr**

    - **Overview**: Fiverr is a freelance marketplace that offers a wide range of services, including book cover design. Designers on Fiverr offer services at various price points, making them accessible to people with different budgets.

    - **Features**:

        o A wide range of designers, from budget-friendly options to high-end professionals.

        o Clear pricing with options for different packages and add-ons.

        o User reviews and ratings to help you choose the right designer.

    - Best for: Authors with a specific budget who want a variety of options at different price points.

4. **Upwork**

    - **Overview**: Upwork is a global freelancing platform where you can hire professionals for a wide range of services, including book design. It's known for its flexibility in terms of hiring and budget.

    - **Features**:

        o Ability to post a job and receive proposals from interested designers.

        o Extensive profiles that include work history, reviews, and portfolio samples.

- o Flexibility in setting the scope, timeline, and budget of your project.

- Best for: Authors who want to take a more hands-on approach to selecting and managing a designer and have the flexibility to negotiate terms directly.

5. **Book Design Templates**

    - **Overview**: While not a freelancer platform, Book Design Templates offers pre-made, professionally designed book cover templates. These can be a cost-effective option if you have some design skills and want to customize a template for your book.

    - **Features**:

        - o Professionally designed templates that are easy to customize.

        - o Affordable pricing for high-quality designs.

        - o Options for both print and digital book covers.

    - Best For: Authors who are comfortable with basic design tools and want a professional look at a lower cost.

6. **Behance**

    - **Overview**: Behance is a portfolio site where designers showcase their work. While it's not a hiring platform per se, you can browse portfolios, find designers whose style you like, and reach out to them directly.

    - **Features**:

        - o Access to a vast array of designers with diverse styles and expertise.

        - o Direct communication with designers to discuss projects.

        - o Ability to see a designer's full range of work, including projects outside of book design.

    - Best For: Authors who are looking for a specific design aesthetic and want to explore a wide range of creative portfolios.

7. **Crowdspring**

    - **Overview**: Crowdspring is a creative marketplace similar to 99designs, where you can run a design contest or hire a designer directly. It focuses on custom design solutions.

- **Features**:
    - Design contests with submissions from multiple designers.
    - One-on-one project options if you prefer to hire a specific designer.
    - Comprehensive portfolios and customer reviews.
- Best For: Authors who want the option of a design contest but also appreciate the ability to work one-on-one with a designer.

8. **DesignCrowd**

- **Overview**: DesignCrowd operates similarly to 99designs, offering both design contests and direct hiring. It's a global platform with a large pool of designers.
- **Features**:
    - Design contests to receive multiple ideas.
    - Direct hire options for working with individual designers.
    - Access to a large, diverse pool of designers.
- Best For: Authors who want to explore a variety of design concepts before making a final decision.

9. **Cover Design Studio**

- **Overview**: Cover Design Studio specializes in book cover design, offering custom designs tailored to your book's genre and audience. It's a more niche service focused exclusively on book covers.
- **Features**:
    - Custom-designed covers that align with industry standards.
    - Experienced designers who specialize in book cover design.
    - Consultation services to ensure the cover meets your vision and market needs.
- Best For Authors looking for a specialized, book-focused design service with a tailored approach.

4. Finalizing the Design: Once you've worked with your designer to create a cover you're happy with, make sure it's optimized for all formats. You'll need versions for print (which include a spine and back cover) and digital formats (which might only require a front cover). Ensure the design looks good in both large formats and as a thumbnail.

Formatting Your Book for Different Platforms

Formatting your book correctly is essential to ensure it looks professional and is easy to read across different devices and platforms.

Print Formatting: For print books, the formatting needs to meet industry standards for physical books.

Choosing between a paperback and a hardcover edition for your book is an important decision that can impact its appeal, pricing, and overall sales strategy. I generally prefer paperback. Here are the pros and cons associated with either option.

1. Cost of Production

- **Paperback**: Generally less expensive to produce than hardcover books. The lower production cost allows for a more affordable retail price, making it accessible to a broader audience.

- **Hardcover**: More expensive to produce due to the higher quality materials and binding process. This results in a higher retail price but also conveys a sense of premium quality and durability.

Consideration: If you're working with a limited budget or want to keep your book's price low to attract more readers, a paperback might be the better option. However, if you can afford the higher production costs, a hardcover edition can help position your book as a premium product.

2. Pricing and Profit Margins

- **Paperback**: Typically sold at a lower price point, which can attract price-sensitive readers. However, the lower price means slimmer profit margins per unit sold.

- **Hardcover**: Priced higher, which can result in higher profit margins per book sold. Readers often perceive hardcover books as more valuable, which can justify the higher price.

Consideration: If you're targeting a market segment that values affordability or if you're aiming for high-volume sales, a paperback might be more suitable. If your target audience is willing to pay more for a premium product, or if you're releasing a special edition, a hardcover might be more appropriate.

3. Target Audience

- **Paperback**: Often preferred by readers who prioritize convenience and portability. Paperbacks are lighter, easier to carry around, and generally favored for casual reading.

- **Hardcover**: Appeals to collectors, libraries, and readers who want a book that feels substantial and durable. Hardcovers are often chosen for books that are considered keepsakes or gifts.

Consideration: Consider who your readers are and what they value. Paperbacks might be more popular for fiction, romance, or genres with a younger audience. For nonfiction, literary fiction, or books aimed at an older or more affluent audience, hardcovers might be the better choice.

4. Market Perception and Positioning

- **Paperback**: Often seen as the more practical, accessible option. If you're aiming for wide distribution and mass-market appeal, paperbacks might help you reach a larger audience.

- **Hardcover**: Generally perceived as more prestigious and high-quality. A hardcover can reinforce that image if you're positioning your book as a serious literary work, a coffee table book, or a collector's item.

Consider how you want your book to be perceived in the marketplace. If you're launching your first book and want to establish yourself as a serious author, a hardcover might help. For follow-up books or less formal works, paperbacks can be a more practical choice.

5. Durability and Longevity

- **Paperbacks** are less durable than hardcovers. They can wear out more quickly, especially with frequent handling, making them less suitable for long-term use or for books intended to be kept as reference materials.

- **Hardcover**: More durable, with better protection for the pages. Hardcovers are more likely to withstand the test of time, making them ideal for books that readers might want to keep on their shelves for years.

If you expect your book to be used frequently or to last for many years (such as reference books, cookbooks, or educational texts), a hardcover might be the better option. If the book is more likely to be read once and then passed on or discarded, a paperback could be sufficient.

6. Release Strategy

- **Paperback**: Often used for initial releases when the goal is to reach as many readers as possible quickly. It can also be released after a hardcover edition to appeal to budget-conscious readers.

- **Hardcover**: Frequently used for first editions, special releases, or to create a sense of exclusivity. Many authors and publishers release a hardcover first, followed by a paperback edition after the initial sales peak.

Consider a staggered release strategy. Start with a hardcover to capitalize on early demand and the desire for a premium product, then release a paperback later to attract a broader audience and prolong the book's sales life.

7. Sales Channels

- **Paperback**: More commonly sold in bookstores, online retailers, and other high-volume outlets. They are often stocked more frequently because of their lower cost and higher turnover rate.

- **Hardcover**: While also sold in bookstores and online, hardcovers are often found in specialty stores, libraries, and higher-end retail locations. They can also be more attractive for author events and book signings.

If you're planning to sell primarily through high-volume retail channels or online platforms, a paperback might be the way to go. If you're targeting niche markets, independent bookstores, or aiming to have your book placed in libraries, a hardcover might be more appropriate.

Here are the key aspects to consider:

- **Trim Size:** Based on your genre and market, choose the appropriate trim size (the dimensions of the book). Common sizes include 5.5" x 8.5" for trade paperbacks and 6" x 9" for fiction.

- **Margins and Bleeds:** Ensure your manuscript has proper margins and bleeds. Bleeds are important if your book includes images that extend to the edge of the page.

- **Typography:** Select a readable font and set appropriate line spacing and paragraph indents. Avoid fonts that are too small or too decorative.

- **Headers, Footers, and Page Numbers:** Include your book title and author name in headers and footers, and ensure that page numbers are correctly placed and formatted.

- **Chapter Breaks:** Use consistent formatting for chapter titles and ensure that each new chapter begins on a new page.

Choosing between a glossy or matte finish

This is an important design decision that affects the book's appearance, feel, and even its marketability.

Here's a breakdown of the factors to consider when deciding between a glossy or matte cover:

1. Visual Appeal

- **Glossy Finish:**

  o Shine and Vibrancy: Glossy covers have a shiny finish, making colors pop and images appear more vibrant. This can be especially effective for books with bold, colorful designs or high-contrast images.

  o Eye-Catching: The reflective surface of a glossy cover can catch the light, making it stand out on shelves or in displays. This can be an advantage in retail settings where you want your book to grab attention quickly.

- **Matte Finish:**

  o Subtle and Elegant: Matte covers have a non-reflective, smooth finish that gives a more understated, sophisticated look. This can work well for literary fiction, non-fiction, or books that aim for a more classic or refined aesthetic.

  o Less Glare: The non-glossy surface of a matte cover reduces glare, making it easier to view the cover design in various lighting conditions.

If your book's design relies on bright colors and images that need to stand out, a glossy finish might be more appropriate. If you're going for a more subtle, elegant look, especially for a text-heavy cover or a design with muted colors, a matte finish might be better.

2. Texture and Feel

- **Glossy Finish:**

  o Smooth and Slick: Glossy covers feel smooth and somewhat slick to the touch. Some readers find this tactile sensation appealing, especially if it complements the book's design and content.

  o Durability: Glossy covers are often more resistant to scratches, smudges, and fingerprints, which can keep the book looking new for longer, especially with frequent handling.

- **Matte Finish:**

  o Soft and Velvety: Matte covers have a softer, almost velvety texture that can give the book a luxurious feel. This texture can add to the overall reading experience and make the book feel more substantial in the reader's hands.

  o Prone to Smudges: Matte covers, while visually appealing, can sometimes show fingerprints or smudges more easily, especially with darker colors. However, some matte finishes have been treated to reduce this issue.

If you want a cover that feels sleek and modern, and you're concerned about durability, a glossy finish may be the way to go. If you prefer a soft, luxurious feel that adds a tactile dimension to the book, a matte finish could be a better choice.

3. Genre and Audience Expectations

- **Glossy Finish:**
    - o Popular Genres: Glossy covers are often used for genres like thrillers, science fiction, fantasy, romance, and children's books, where bright colors and dynamic images are common.
    - o Audience Appeal: Readers of these genres may expect a vibrant, glossy finish that matches the tone and excitement of the content.

- **Matte Finish:**
    - o Popular Genres: Matte covers are frequently used for literary fiction, memoirs, non-fiction, and certain types of art or photography books, where a more sophisticated, understated appearance is preferred.
    - o Audience Appeal: Readers who gravitate towards these genres may appreciate the elegance and subtlety of a matte finish.

Consider what readers in your genre typically expect and respond to. Aligning your cover finish with genre conventions can help meet reader expectations and improve the book's appeal.

4. Practical Considerations

- **Glossy Finish:**
    - o Durability: Glossy covers are more resistant to wear and tear, making them a good choice for books that will be frequently handled or displayed in environments where durability is important.
    - o Cleaning: Glossy covers can be wiped clean more easily, which can be a practical advantage for books that will be handled by many people, such as in bookstores or libraries.

- **Matte Finish:**
    - o Wear and Tear: Matte covers can show signs of wear more quickly, especially on the edges and corners. However, some readers and collectors appreciate the "well-loved" look that matte covers can develop over time.
    - o Environmental Factors: Matte covers might absorb more oils from hands or environmental elements, which could affect their appearance over time.

If your book will be subjected to heavy handling or you're particularly concerned about long-term durability, a glossy finish may offer better protection. If you're more focused on aesthetics and the sensory experience, and the book won't be heavily handled, a matte finish could be ideal.

5. Printing and Costs

- **Glossy Finish:** Generally, there's little to no difference in cost between glossy and matte finishes, though this can vary depending on your printer or publisher. Glossy finishes might sometimes cost slightly more if extra treatments or coatings are applied.

- **Matte Finish:** Matte finishes are often priced similarly to glossy finishes, but again, this can depend on the specific treatments or finishes offered by your printer.

While cost differences are usually minimal, it's worth checking with your printer to ensure there are no unexpected fees associated with your chosen finish.

6. Ebook Formatting:

Ebooks require different formatting considerations to ensure they display correctly on various devices, such as Kindles, tablets, and smartphones.

- **Reflowable Text:** Ebooks use reflowable text, meaning the content adjusts to fit the screen size. Avoid fixed layouts and ensure your text can reflow without breaking the reading experience.

- **Table of Contents:** Include a clickable table of contents that allows readers to navigate easily through the ebook.

- **Hyperlinks:** Use hyperlinks for any references, external websites, or navigation within the book.

- **Images**: Ensure that images are optimized for digital use, with appropriate resolution and file size, to prevent slow loading times.

- **File Formats:** Common ebook formats include EPUB (used by most platforms) and MOBI (used by Amazon's Kindle). Make sure your book is available in the appropriate format for each platform.

7. Tools and Services:

- **Formatting Software:** Tools like Scrivener, Vellum, and Reedsy Book Editor offer user-friendly options for formatting both print and digital books.

- **Professional Formatting Services:** If you prefer to avoid handling formatting yourself, consider hiring a professional formatter who can ensure your book meets all industry standards.

Setting the Right Price

Pricing your book correctly is a crucial aspect of your self-publishing strategy. The right price can attract readers, maximize sales, and ensure you receive a fair return on your work. Here's how to determine the best pricing strategy for your book.

1. **Research the Market:** Start by researching the prices of similar books in your genre. Look at both bestsellers and mid-list titles to get a sense of the standard price range. Consider factors such as the length of the book, the author's reputation, and whether the book is part of a series.

2. **Ebook Pricing:** Ebook pricing is often lower than print book pricing, but it varies based on several factors:

    - Pricing Tiers: Common ebook price points include $0.99, $2.99, and $4.99. Pricing your ebook at $2.99 or above often qualifies you for higher royalty rates on platforms like Amazon KDP (typically 70%).

    - Promotional Pricing: To generate buzz and increase visibility, consider using promotional pricing strategies, such as offering your book for free or at a discounted rate for a limited time.

    - Value Perception: Be mindful that pricing an ebook too low might devalue it in the eyes of potential readers. Conversely, pricing it too high could deter readers from taking a chance on an unknown author.

3. **Print Book Pricing:** Print books typically have higher production costs, which need to be factored into the price.

    - **Cost of Production:** Calculate the cost of printing each book (including cover, binding, and paper quality) and set a price that covers these costs while providing a reasonable profit margin.

    - **Perceived Value:** Consider the perceived value of a physical book. Readers are often willing to pay more for a well-designed, professionally produced print book.

    - **Genre Considerations:** Different genres have different pricing expectations. For example, non-fiction books often command higher prices than fiction due to the specialized knowledge they contain.

4. **Dynamic Pricing:** Be open to adjusting your book's price based on its performance and market conditions. Some authors use dynamic pricing strategies, where the price changes over time based on demand, sales data, and promotional efforts.

5. **Royalties and Revenue:** Understand how pricing affects your royalties. Most platforms have tiered royalty rates based on the price of your book. For example, Amazon KDP offers a 70% royalty rate for ebooks priced between $2.99 and $9.99 but only 35% for books priced outside this range.

6. **Bundling and Discounts:** Consider offering bundled deals or discounts for purchasing multiple books, especially if you have a series. Bundling can increase the perceived value for readers and boost overall sales.

Chapter 13
Marketing Your Book

Publishing your book is only the first step in your journey to success as an author. Marketing is crucial to ensure that your book reaches its intended audience and achieves its full potential. Regardless of which route you take in publishing your book, self-publishing or a traditional publisher, start building your author profile as early as possible in as many places as you can. At least three months in advance, especially if you want to do podcasts, radio, TV, and live events. Promoting these events and building momentum early will help build your audience.

Engage with other writers, especially in your genre. Engage with people who are interested in your topic or genre on social media and other platforms like Goodreads Groups, Bookish, Bookclubz, Discord (book-related servers), Facebook Groups (book clubs and author communities), The StoryGraph (community features), Fable, Reddit (book-related subreddits), Telegram (book-related channels and groups), Slack (book club channels).

Building an Author Platform

What is an Author Platform? An author platform is your presence, reputation, and visibility as an author. It's the foundation upon which you can build a readership, engage with fans, and promote your books. An author platform can include your website, blog, email list, social media profiles, and any other channels through which you connect with your audience. Don't leave out networking in person and through groups and organizations aligned with your book!

Key Components of an Author Platform:

- **Website/Blog:** Your author website serves as the central hub of your platform. It should include a professional bio, information about your books, a blog (if relevant), and a way for readers to subscribe to your email list. However, these days, this isn't as critical as it used to be and can be an expense you skip if you use a platform like Substack or any other service that allows you to collect emails from your readers and communicate directly with them.

- **Email List:** An email list allows you to communicate directly with your readers. Use it to share news about upcoming releases, exclusive content, and promotions. Offering a free ebook or short story as an incentive can help you grow your list.

- **Social Media Profiles:** Platforms like Twitter, Facebook, Instagram, and LinkedIn are valuable tools for building your brand, engaging with readers, and promoting your work. Engage with genre-specific groups and pages to connect with people who would likely read your book. It's not just about overt promotion; it's about being engaged with the community, which can lead to potential followers and readers.

- **Amazon Author Page and Other Branded Pages:**

    o **Amazon Author Page:** Amazon offers a dedicated author page where you can showcase all your books, share your biography, post updates, and connect with readers. Setting up a comprehensive Amazon Author Page is crucial as it consolidates all your works in one place, making it easier for readers to find you. It also provides analytics about your books' performance and allows you to add a blog feed and other media to enhance your brand.

    o **Goodreads Author Page:** Goodreads allows authors to create a profile where they can list their books, write a blog, host giveaways, and interact with readers directly through reviews and group discussions. It's a great way to engage with an active community of book lovers.

    o **BookBub Author Profile:** BookBub offers authors a profile where they can connect with readers who follow their updates, share book recommendations, and promote new releases and deals. Followers on BookBub are notified whenever you release a new book, which can be an excellent way to boost initial sales.

    o **Barnes & Noble Author Page:** Similar to Amazon, Barnes & Noble allows authors to create a branded page that lists all their books, includes their biography, and connects them with readers through promotional opportunities.

    o **Kobo Writing Life Author Page:** Kobo's platform lets you create an author page, link all your published books, and reach a global audience. It's particularly beneficial for international markets outside of the U.S.

- **Outside Blogging on Platforms like Medium, Substack, and Patreon:**

    o **Medium**: Medium is a popular blogging platform where you can publish articles to a wide audience. It's great for building authority and connecting with readers interested in your genre or topics related to your book. You can join the Medium Partner Program to earn money based on the engagement your articles receive.

    o **Substack**: Substack is an email newsletter platform that allows you to build a dedicated subscriber base. You can offer free or paid subscriptions and directly engage with your readers through regular updates, essays, or serialized content. It's a great way to develop a loyal following and create a direct line of communication with your audience.

    o **Patreon**: Patreon is a membership platform where your followers can support you through monthly subscriptions. It's ideal for offering exclusive content, such as early chapters, bonus material, or behind-the-scenes updates. It provides an additional income stream and fosters a close-knit community around your work.

By leveraging these external blogging platforms, you can expand your reach beyond your website and build a dedicated following, grow your email list, and potentially create additional revenue streams, all while positioning yourself as an active, engaged author in your genre or niche.

Writing on platforms like Substack and Medium

Writing on sites like this can be incredibly beneficial for building your author profile, reaching new audiences, and establishing your expertise in a particular niche. Here's how these platforms can help you grow your presence as an author: (There are other genre-specific platforms you can also look at.)

1. Building an Audience

Substack:

- Email List Growth: Substack allows you to build a dedicated email subscriber list. Each time you publish a piece, it's sent directly to your subscribers' inboxes, which helps you maintain a direct connection with your readers. Over time, this list can become one of your most valuable assets for promoting your books and other content.

- Targeted Audience: Since readers subscribe based on their interest in your specific content, the audience you build on Substack is highly targeted and engaged, making them more likely to be interested in your books and other writings.

Medium:

- Broad Reach: Medium has a built-in audience of millions of readers who actively engage with content on the platform. By publishing on Medium, you can reach a large and diverse audience, many of whom may not have discovered you otherwise.

- Discoverability: Medium's algorithms and tags help surface your content to readers interested in topics you write about, increasing the chances of your work being discovered by a wider audience.

2. Establishing Authority and Expertise

Substack:

- Niche Focus: Substack is particularly effective for building a profile in a specific niche. By consistently publishing high-quality content in your area of expertise, you can position yourself as a thought leader or authority in that field. This can be especially beneficial if your books are non-fiction or focused on a particular subject.

- Long-Form Content: Substack supports long-form writing, allowing you to delve deeply into topics, share detailed insights, and provide value to your readers, which helps reinforce your credibility.

Medium:

- Wide Range of Topics: Medium's diverse readership means you can write on a variety of topics and still reach an interested audience. Whether you write about writing, personal development, technology, or any other subject, you can establish yourself as an expert in that area.

- Featured and Curation Opportunities: Medium's editorial team often curates articles to feature on the homepage or in topic-specific newsletters. Being featured can significantly boost your visibility and establish you as a reputable voice on the platform.

Submitting to magazines and news outlets.

A wonderful way to build your platform and credibility as a writer is to submit essays, etc., to different publications. Especially ones that fit your genre or topic. Think a little outside of the box in terms of direct correlation to your work. You can expand your audience by understanding the demo/psychographics of a publication. It's likely you will find more readers by submitting essays, etc., that may include your topic (Don't blog your book- i.e., don't submit chapters or say the same things as your book in the same way)

Here are some suggestions. You can find many genre-specific outlets.

1. The New Yorker

- What they accept: Fiction, nonfiction, poetry, and essays.
- Website: https://www.newyorker.com
- Submission link: Fiction/Poetry submissions

2. The Sun Magazine

- What they accept: Personal essays, interviews, poetry, and short stories.
- Website: https://www.thesunmagazine.org
- Submission link: Submit here

3. Narratively

- What they accept: Personal essays and long-form storytelling on a wide range of topics.
- Website: https://www.narratively.com
- Submission link: Pitch here

4. Tin House

- What they accept: Fiction, nonfiction, and poetry.
- Website: https://tinhouse.com
- Submission link: Submit here

5. Vox First Person

- What they accept: First-person essays on contemporary issues.
- Website: https://www.vox.com
- Submission link: Pitch via email

6. HuffPost Personal

- What they accept: Personal essays on relationships, family, personal growth, and more.
- Website: https://www.huffpost.com
- Submission link: Pitch via email

7. **Longreads**

    - What they accept: Longform essays and narrative journalism.
    - Website: https://longreads.com
    - Submission link: Pitch via email

8. **The Rumpus**

    - What they accept: Personal essays, interviews, and literary criticism.
    - Website: https://therumpus.net
    - Submission link: Submit here

9. **Creative Nonfiction**

    - What they accept: Personal essays and narrative nonfiction.
    - Website: https://www.creativenonfiction.org
    - Submission link: Submit here

10. **Brevity**

    - What they accept: Flash nonfiction essays (750 words or fewer).
    - Website: https://brevitymag.com
    - Submission link: Submit here

11. **The Boston Globe - Connections**

    - What they accept: Short essays about relationships.
    - Website: https://www.bostonglobe.com
    - Submission link: Submit via email

12. **New York Times - Tiny Love Stories**

    - What they accept: Very short essays (100 words) about love and relationships.
    - Website: https://www.nytimes.com/column/modern-love
    - Submission link: Submit here

13. **Slice Magazine**

    - What they accept: Fiction, nonfiction, and poetry.
    - Website: https://slicemagazine.org
    - Submission link: Submit here

14. The Threepenny Review

- What they accept: Short stories, personal essays, memoirs, and poetry.

- Website: https://www.threepennyreview.com

- Submission link: Submit here

15. Salon

- What they accept: Personal essays with a cultural or political angle.

- Website: https://www.salon.com

- Submission link: Pitch via email

3. Driving Book Sales and Promotions

Substack:

- Direct Promotion: With your own email list on Substack, you can directly promote your books, upcoming releases, and special offers to your subscribers. This direct line of communication is incredibly valuable for driving sales, especially during book launches.

- Exclusive Content: You can offer exclusive content, such as behind-the-scenes looks at your writing process, early chapters, or special essays, to entice subscribers. This can create a loyal reader base that is more likely to support your book sales.

Medium:

- Links and CTAs: Medium allows you to include links to your books and other works within your articles. You can use calls-to-action (CTAs) at the end of your posts to encourage readers to check out your books or subscribe to your newsletter.

- Storytelling and Excerpts: Medium is a great platform for sharing excerpts from your books, short stories, or related essays that can pique readers' interest in your full-length works.

4. Networking and Collaboration

Substack:

- Collaborative Opportunities: By connecting with other writers and creators on Substack, you can collaborate on newsletters, cross-promote each other's work, or co-author articles. This can help you reach new audiences and build relationships within your niche or genre.

- Community Building: Substack allows you to create a community around your writing. Engaging with your subscribers through comments, Q&A sessions, or subscriber-only posts can strengthen your relationship with your readers and make them more invested in your success.

Medium:

- Publications and Communities: Medium features numerous publications that accept submissions from writers. Being published in a popular Medium publication can expose your work to a much larger audience and help you connect with other writers and editors in your field.

- Reader Interaction: Medium's comment and highlight features allow readers to engage directly with your content. This interaction can provide valuable feedback, help you refine your ideas, and build a network of engaged readers and fellow writers.

5. Monetization Opportunities

Substack:

- Subscription Revenue: Substack offers the ability to monetize your writing through paid subscriptions. If you build a substantial audience, you can offer premium content to subscribers who pay a monthly or yearly fee. This can provide a steady stream of income and further incentivize you to produce high-quality content.

- Paid Newsletters: By offering paid newsletters with exclusive content, you can generate additional revenue while providing extra value to your most dedicated readers.

Medium:

- Medium Partner Program: Medium's Partner Program allows you to earn money based on the engagement your stories receive from Medium members. While it may not generate substantial income initially, it's a nice bonus for content you're already creating.

- Membership Growth: As you gain followers on Medium, you can encourage them to join your Substack newsletter, where you can offer paid content or exclusive deals on your books.

Here are some other platforms to consider: Patreon, Ghost, Vocal, HubPages, NewsBreak, LinkedIn Articles, Revue, Wattpad, Medium Partner Program, Mirror.xyz.

Social Media Strategies

Social media is a powerful tool for connecting with readers and promoting your book. However, success on social media requires a strategic approach.

If you intend to hire a social media marketing company or person, remember to have the conversation about requirements, needs, wants, and everyone's expectations. Have them clearly outline their scope of work and all costs associated with working with them. Create a list of benchmarks/goals and a timeline to achieve them.

Choosing the Right Platforms:

- **Twitter**: Great for real-time updates, networking with other writers, and participating in hashtag events like #WritingCommunity.

- **Facebook**: Useful for building communities through author pages and groups. Facebook ads can also be an effective way to reach specific audiences.

- **Instagram**: Ideal for sharing visually appealing content like book covers, quotes, and behind-the-scenes glimpses into your writing process. Instagram Stories and IGTV can enhance engagement.

- **TikTok**: Increasingly popular for book promotion, especially through the #BookTok community. Short, creative videos can go viral and significantly boost your book's visibility.

Content Strategies:

- **Consistency is Key:** Post regularly to keep your audience engaged. Develop a content calendar to plan your posts in advance.

- **Engage with Your Audience:** Respond to comments and messages, and engage with your followers' content as well. Building relationships is crucial on social media.

- **Share a Mix of Content:** Combine promotional posts with personal updates, writing tips, book recommendations, and reader interactions to keep your feed varied and interesting.

- **Use Hashtags:** Research and use relevant hashtags to increase the visibility of your posts. Popular hashtags in the writing community include #amwriting, #bookstagram, #booktok, and #authorsofinstagram.

Running Book Promotions and Giveaways

Promotions and giveaways are effective ways to generate excitement, build your readership, and boost sales.

Book Promotions:

- Discounted Pricing: Offer your ebook at a discounted price or even free for a limited time. Use platforms like BookBub, Kindle Countdown Deals, or Freebooksy to reach a broader audience.

- Bundling: If you have multiple books, consider bundling them together at a special price. This encourages readers to buy more than one book at a time.

- Pre-Order Campaigns: Encourage readers to pre-order your book by offering exclusive content or discounts for early buyers.

Giveaways:

- Why Giveaways Work: Giveaways generate buzz and create opportunities for readers to discover your work. They can also help you grow your email list and social media following.

- Types of Giveaways: Offer signed copies, merchandise, or digital bundles—partner with other authors or book bloggers to amplify your reach.

- Hosting Giveaways: Use platforms like Goodreads, Rafflecopter, or your own social media channels to host and promote your giveaway. Make the entry process simple, like following your social media account, joining your email list, or sharing the giveaway post.

Live Author Events and Speaking Engagements

In-person and virtual events are excellent ways to connect with readers, build your brand, and promote your book.

In-Person Events:

- Book Signings: Host signings at local bookstores, libraries, or literary festivals. Promote these events on your social media and through local media outlets.

- Workshops and Readings: Offer workshops, readings, or discussions about your book's themes or writing process. These can be held at bookstores, community centers, or literary conferences.

- Collaborate with Local Businesses: Partner with local businesses or cafes to host a book launch event or reading. This can attract local readers and create a buzz in your community.

Virtual Events:

- Webinars and Live Streams: Use platforms like Zoom, Facebook Live, or YouTube to host virtual book launches, Q&A sessions, or writing workshops. This allows you to reach a global audience.

- Podcast Appearances: Guest on podcasts related to your book's genre or subject matter. This can introduce your book to a new audience and establish you as an expert in your field.

- Virtual Book Clubs: Participate in or organize virtual book clubs that feature your book. Engage with readers through discussions and Q&A sessions.

PR and Traditional Advertising

Public relations (PR) and traditional advertising can complement your digital marketing efforts and help you reach a broader audience.

PR Strategies:

- Press Releases: Write and distribute press releases to announce your book launch, awards, or events. Use PR distribution services like PR Newswire or pitch directly to local media outlets.

- Media Coverage: Pitch your book to newspapers, magazines, radio stations, and TV shows. Focus on angles that tie into your book's current events, local interest, or unique aspects.

- Book Reviews: Submit your book to reputable review sites, book bloggers, and literary magazines. Positive reviews can enhance your credibility and boost sales.

Traditional Advertising:

- Print Ads: Place ads in local newspapers, magazines, or literary journals that cater to your target audience.

- Radio and Podcast Ads: Purchase ad slots on radio stations or podcasts that align with your book's genre or themes.

- Bookstore Displays: Negotiate with bookstores for featured placement, such as endcap displays or window promotions.

Estimated Marketing Budget

Here is an estimated – bare-bones budget for marketing your book:

Marketing Budget for a Self-Published Book ($5,000)

1. **Book Cover Design and Branding: $500**

    o   Professional cover design: $300

    o   Branding elements (social media banners, logos, etc.): $200

2. **Author Website: $800 (This is optional, in my opinion – unless you are building a brand with multiple offerings)**

    o   Website design and development: $600

    o   Domain registration and hosting: $100

    o   SEO optimization and plugins: $100

3. **Social Media Advertising: $1,200**

    o   Facebook/Instagram ads: $600

    o   Twitter ads: $300

    o   Pinterest ads: $300

4. **4Email Marketing: $300**

    o   Email marketing service (Mailchimp, ConvertKit, etc.): $150

    o   Lead magnet design (e.g., free ebook or guide): $150

5. **Book Review Services: $400**

    o   Paid review services (Kirkus Reviews, IndieReader, etc.): $300

    o   Advance Review Copy (ARC) distribution (NetGalley or similar): $100

6. **Promotional Campaigns: $1,000**

    o   BookBub or similar promotional services: $600

    o   Goodreads giveaway: $200

    o   Paid newsletter promotions (e.g., Freebooksy, Bargain Booksy): $200

7. **Public Relations (PR): $500**

    o   Press release distribution: $200

    o   Podcast and blog tour: $200

    o   Media kit creation: $100

8. **Live Events and Book Launch: $300**

    o   Virtual book launch event: $100

    o   Local book signing event: $200 (includes venue, marketing materials, etc.)

Total Budget: $5,000

When to Launch

The best day and month to launch your book can vary depending on the genre, audience, and marketing strategy. Here's a general guide:

Best Months to Launch by Genre:

1. **Fiction (General, Literary, Romance, Historical):**

    o   Best Months: March, April, September, October

    o   Why: These months are strong for fiction because they precede major book-buying seasons—spring (before summer reading) and fall (before the holiday season). Literary awards often occur in the fall, making it a strategic time to launch literary fiction.

2. **Mystery, Thriller, and Crime:**

    o   Best Months: September, October

    o   Why: These genres align well with the fall season, leading into Halloween. Readers are looking for darker, suspenseful reads as the nights get longer.

3. **Science Fiction and Fantasy:**

    o   Best Months: May, July, November

    o   Why: May and July work well as they coincide with major fan conventions (like Comic-Con) and summer reading. November is good for holiday gift purchases, particularly for new series or anticipated sequels.

4. **Non-Fiction (Business, Self-Help, Memoir, Biography):**

    o   Best Months: January, September

- o   Why: January is ideal for self-help and business books due to New Year's resolutions. September works well as people return from summer vacations and are ready to refocus on personal development and learning.

5. **Young Adult (YA):**

   - o   Best Months: March, June, October

   - o   Why: March is good for spring break reads, June for summer vacations, and October aligns with back-to-school season and Halloween (especially for fantasy or paranormal YA).

6. **Children's Books:**

   - o   Best Months: August, November

   - o   Why: August is great for back-to-school promotions, and November is ideal for the holiday season when parents and relatives are looking for gifts.

7. **Horror:**

   - o   Best Months: September, October

   - o   Why: The lead-up to Halloween is perfect for horror as readers seek out spooky stories.

8. **Cookbooks and Lifestyle:**

   - o   Best Months: October, November

   - o   Why: These genres sell well leading up to the holiday season when people are planning gatherings and looking for gifts.

Best Days to Launch:

- Tuesday: Traditionally, Tuesday is the most common day for book launches in the publishing industry. It gives books a full week to build sales and rankings before weekend reports.

- Wednesday/Thursday are also good options, especially if Tuesday is crowded with other major releases. These days still allow for a full week of promotion leading into the weekend.

Key Considerations:

- **Avoid Major Holidays:** Unless your book is specifically themed around a holiday, it's best to avoid launching close to major holidays when people are less likely to be focused on book buying.

- **Consider Genre Trends:** Some genres may have specific trends or events that are worth aligning with, such as National Novel Writing Month (NaNoWriMo) in November for fiction writers or Back-to-School season for educational and children's books.

- **Seasonal Relevance:** Think about the seasonal appeal of your book. A summer beach read might do better if launched in late spring, while a cozy mystery might be better suited for fall.

Chapter 14
Distribution and Sales

Successfully distributing and selling your book is just as crucial as writing it. Whether you're targeting bookstore shelves, online marketplaces, or library catalogs, understanding the distribution channels and sales strategies available to you will play a significant role in your book's success. Most of your sales will likely come from online platforms, or events, where you appear in person, so having a solid strategy for both, is essential.

While everyone dreams of becoming a best-selling author, especially on platforms like Amazon, you don't need to spend a fortune to achieve this status. Instead, focus on leveraging your platform and enlisting the support of your friends, family, and network. Creating a solid buzz around your book, especially on your launch day, is vital in securing that coveted best-seller spot.

To prepare for a successful launch, develop email templates, social media copy, images, and graphics that your friends and colleagues can easily share. Include everything they might need, such as suggested hashtags, sample messages, and even fun graphics or GIFs to make sharing your book more engaging. Encourage everyone in your circle to help promote your book, and be specific in your requests to make it as easy as possible for them to support you.

Create a dedicated link for your book using Bit.ly or another link-tracking platform to measure traffic to your Amazon book page. Ensure your Amazon Author Page is set up and optimized before the launch. Ask everyone to purchase from your dedicated link during the crucial 3-5 day window following your launch to maximize your sales ranking.

When setting up your book on Amazon, carefully choose your categories. This is crucial for achieving Amazon's Best-Seller status. Select one primary category that is directly relevant to your book, even if it's highly competitive. Then, also choose relevant secondary categories that may have less competition, increasing your chances of ranking higher in those areas.

Best-Seller Campaigns and General Sales

In addition to these steps, consider implementing the following strategies:

- **Host a Virtual Launch Event**: Plan an online book launch party or Q&A session on platforms like Zoom, Facebook Live, or Instagram Live to engage with your audience and encourage them to buy your book during the event.

- **Collaborate with Other Authors or Influencers:** Partner with authors in your genre or influencers with a similar audience to cross-promote your book. You can arrange guest blog posts, joint live sessions, or social media shoutouts to reach a wider audience.

- **Submit Your Book to Book Reviewers and Bloggers:** Contact book reviewers, bloggers, and influencers to request reviews, interviews, or features. Positive reviews and media coverage can drive significant traffic and boost sales.

- **Offer Limited-Time Promotions or Discounts:** To incentivize purchases and drive sales momentum, consider offering a special launch week discount or bundling your book with related content (like a free chapter, a guide, or a downloadable resource).

- **Build Your Email List:** If you haven't already, create a landing page for your book on your website or blog to capture emails from interested readers. Send exclusive updates, sneak peeks, or behind-the-scenes content to keep them engaged and ready to buy on launch day.

By strategically planning your launch and utilizing a variety of promotional tactics, you'll maximize your book's visibility, sales, and overall success. Remember, it's about creating excitement, leveraging your network, and making it easy for others to support you in your journey to becoming a best-selling author!

Getting Your Book into Bookstores and Libraries

1. Approaching Bookstores:

- **Establishing Distribution Channels:** To get your book into brick-and-mortar bookstores, you'll need to ensure it's available through a major distributor like Ingram or Baker & Taylor. These distributors have established relationships with bookstores, making ordering and stocking your book easier.

- **Pitching to Bookstores:** Start with local independent bookstores. Prepare a professional pitch with a sell sheet with key details such as your book's ISBN, cover image, brief description, and notable endorsements. Highlight any local ties or relevance to the store's customer base.

- **Consignment Agreements:** Some independent bookstores might offer consignment deals, where they stock your book and pay you only when it sells. This can be a good way to get your foot in the door.

- **Bookstore Events:** Hosting a reading or book signing at a bookstore can help boost your book's presence and sales. Events create a buzz and give you a chance to connect with potential readers personally.

2. Getting Your Book into Libraries:

- **Library Distribution Services:** Services like OverDrive, which specializes in distributing digital content to libraries, can help get your ebook into libraries. For print books, having your book available through Ingram or Baker & Taylor is also essential.

- **Approaching Libraries Directly:** Just like bookstores, you can approach libraries directly, especially local ones. Offer to donate a copy or participate in an author event to increase your chances of getting your book on their shelves.

- **Library Journals:** Submitting your book for review in library journals like Library Journal, Booklist, or Kirkus can increase the likelihood of libraries stocking it. Librarians highly regard positive reviews in these publications.

Maximizing Online Sales – marketing channels

1. Choosing the Right Platforms:

- **Amazon:** As the largest online bookseller, Amazon is a crucial platform for any author. Ensure your book is listed with a compelling product page that includes a well-written description, a professional cover image, and a competitive price.

- **Other Retailers:** Don't overlook platforms like Barnes & Noble, Apple Books, Kobo, and Google Play. Listing your book on multiple platforms increases your reach and accessibility to different reader demographics.

- **Your Own Website:** Selling directly from your website can offer higher profit margins and a direct connection to your readers. Use your website to offer special editions, signed copies, or bundles that aren't available elsewhere. **Note-** if you sell directly from your website, be prepared to store and ship inventory. I don't recommend this option unless you are already selling other products.

2. Online Advertising:

- **Amazon Ads:** Use Amazon's advertising platform to target potential readers based on their browsing and buying habits. Sponsored products and keyword-targeted ads can significantly boost your book's visibility.

- **Social Media Ads:** Platforms like Facebook, Instagram, and Twitter allow you to target ads to specific demographics, interests, and behaviors, making it easier to reach potential readers who are likely to be interested in your book.

- **Book Promotion Services:** Consider using services like BookBub, which can send out targeted promotions to large audiences of dedicated readers, boosting your book's visibility and sales.

Leveraging Reviews and Reader Feedback

1. Importance of Reviews:

- **Social Proof:** Reviews serve as social proof, helping potential readers decide whether your book is worth their time. A substantial number of positive reviews can significantly influence buying decisions.

- **Algorithm Boost:** On platforms like Amazon, books with more reviews are often given higher visibility in search results and recommendation algorithms.

2. Strategies for Getting Reviews:

- **Advance Review Copies (ARCs):** Distribute ARCs to book bloggers, influencers, and early readers to gather reviews before your book's official launch. Use services like NetGalley to reach a broader audience of reviewers.

- **Ask Your Readers:** Encourage readers to leave reviews at the end of your book or in your email newsletter. Sometimes, a simple request is enough to generate more reviews.

- **Book Review Services:** Consider submitting your book to paid review services like Kirkus Reviews or IndieReader. These services provide professional, in-depth reviews that can be used in your marketing materials.

3. Handling Negative Feedback:

- **Stay Professional:** Negative reviews are inevitable, but it's important to handle them professionally. Avoid responding defensively or arguing with reviewers. Instead, learn from constructive criticism and use it to improve future work.

- **Balancing Reviews:** A mix of positive and negative reviews can actually make your book seem more credible. Potential readers may be skeptical of a book that only has glowing reviews, so a few critical perspectives can provide a balanced view.

Utilizing Endorsements

1. **The Power of Endorsements:**

   - **Credibility Boost:** Endorsements from well-known authors, industry experts, or influencers can significantly boost your book's credibility. They serve as a stamp of approval, helping to convince potential readers that your book is worth their time and money.

   - **Marketing Leverage:** Use endorsements in your marketing materials, including your book cover, product page, press releases, and social media. A strong endorsement can be a key selling point.

2. **How to Get Endorsements:**

   - **Targeted Requests:** Reach out to authors, influencers, or experts who are familiar with your genre or subject matter. Personalize your request, explaining why you believe they would appreciate your book and how their endorsement would be valuable.

   - **Leverage Your Network:** If you have connections within the publishing industry, use them to request endorsements. Sometimes, a mutual contact can facilitate an introduction.

   - **Offer Early Copies:** Send potential endorsers an early copy of your book, along with a polite request for a blurb or endorsement if they enjoy it.

3. **Maximizing the Impact of Endorsements:**

   - **Highlight on Your Cover:** If you receive a strong endorsement from a well-known figure, consider placing it prominently on your book's cover.

   - **Use in Marketing:** Feature endorsements in all your promotional materials, including your website, social media, email newsletters, and advertisements. Endorsements can be a powerful tool in convincing new readers to give your book a try.

Part 5:
Beyond the Book

Chapter 15
Legal and Financial Considerations

Navigating the legal and financial aspects of writing can seem daunting, but understanding these key areas is essential for establishing a sustainable and professional writing career. For the record, I am not a lawyer or an accountant. I strongly advise you to consult with and engage, when necessary, legal counsel and an accountant. Here are some things to consider.

Copyrights and Trademarks

1. Understanding Copyright:

1. **What is Copyright?**
   - Copyright is a legal protection that grants the creator of an original work exclusive rights to use, distribute, and license their work. This protection applies to literary, musical, artistic, and certain other intellectual works.

- **Automatic Protection:**
   - In most countries, including the United States, copyright protection is automatic upon the creation of your work in a tangible form. This means that as soon as you write your book, it is protected under copyright law.

- **Rights Granted by Copyright:**
   - As the copyright holder, you have the exclusive rights to reproduce the work, create derivative works, distribute copies, publicly perform, and display the

work. You can also transfer these rights, either in whole or in part, through licensing agreements.

- **Registering Your Copyright:**
    - While registration is not required to claim copyright protection, it offers significant benefits, including the ability to file a lawsuit for infringement and the potential to recover statutory damages and attorney's fees. In the U.S., you can register your copyright through the U.S. Copyright Office.

2. **Understanding Trademarks:**

- **What is a Trademark?**
    - A trademark is a symbol, word, or phrase legally registered or established by use as representing a company or product. For authors, trademarks can apply to a series title, pen name, or even a unique branding element associated with **your work.**

- **Why Trademarks Matter:**
    - Trademarks protect your brand identity and prevent others from using a name or logo that could confuse consumers or dilute your brand. For example, if you're writing a series of books under a unique title, trademarking that title can prevent others from using it.

- **Registering a Trademark:**
    - In the U.S., you can register a trademark through the United States Patent and Trademark Office (USPTO). The process involves conducting a search to ensure the name isn't already in use, filing an application, and paying the required fees.

3. **Protecting Your Work:**

- **Monitoring for Infringement:**
    - Once you've secured your copyrights and trademarks, it's important to monitor for potential infringements. This can include regularly searching for unauthorized copies of your work online or keeping an eye on new publications that may use similar branding.

- **Taking Action:**
    - If you discover an infringement, consider sending a cease-and-desist letter as a first step. In cases of significant infringement, you may need to consult with an intellectual property attorney to explore legal action.

Taxes and Accounting for Writers

1. Understanding Your Tax Obligations:

- **Income Tax:**
  - As a writer, your book sales, royalties, and any other income you earn from your writing are considered taxable income. It's important to keep accurate records of all your earnings, as well as any deductions you're entitled to claim.

- **Self-Employment Tax:**
  - If you're earning income as a self-employed writer, you may also be subject to self-employment tax, which covers Social Security and Medicare taxes. This applies even if you're only writing part-time.

- **Quarterly Estimated Taxes:**
  - Self-employed individuals, including writers, are typically required to pay estimated taxes on a quarterly basis. This is because your income is not subject to withholding, unlike traditional employment. Failing to pay quarterly taxes can result in penalties.

2. Deductions and Write-Offs:

- **Home Office Deduction:**
  - If you have a dedicated space in your home that you use exclusively for writing, you may be eligible for the home office deduction. This allows you to deduct a portion of your rent or mortgage, utilities, and other expenses.

- **Business Expenses:**
  - Common deductible expenses for writers include supplies (like computers, software, and stationery), research materials (books, subscriptions), marketing and promotional costs, and travel expenses related to your writing activities.

- **Professional Services:**
  - Fees paid to editors, graphic designers, lawyers, or accountants can also be deducted as business expenses as long as they are directly related to your writing business.

3. Record Keeping and Accounting:

- **Tracking Income and Expenses:**
  - Keeping meticulous records is crucial for tax purposes. Use accounting software like QuickBooks or even simple spreadsheets to track your income and expenses

throughout the year. This will make tax season much easier and help ensure you claim all eligible deductions.

- **Hiring an Accountant:**
  - If your finances are complex, consider hiring an accountant who specializes in working with creatives or small business owners. They can help you navigate the tax code, identify potential deductions, and ensure you comply with all tax obligations.

Setting Up a Writing Business

1. Choosing a Business Structure:

- **Sole Proprietorship:**
  - Most writers start out as sole proprietors, meaning there's no legal distinction between the business and the individual. This is the simplest and most common business structure for writers, but it also means you're personally liable for any business debts or legal actions.

- **Limited Liability Company (LLC):**
  - An LLC provides greater protection by separating your personal and business assets. This can be a good option if you have significant income from your writing or are collaborating with other writers who want to limit your liability.

- **Corporation:**
  - Forming a corporation is less common for individual writers due to the complexity and cost involved. However, it may be worth considering if you plan to expand your business significantly, hire employees, or seek outside investment.

2. Registering Your Business:

- **Business Name Registration:**
  - If you're operating under a name other than your own (e.g., a pen name or a brand name for your writing business), you'll need to register that name with your local government. This is often referred to as filing a "Doing Business As" (DBA) name.

- **Obtaining an EIN:**
  - An Employer Identification Number (EIN) is required if you plan to hire employees, form an LLC or corporation, or operate as a partnership. You can obtain an EIN from the IRS at no cost.

3. **Managing Business Operations:**

- **Bank Accounts:**

   o   Open a separate business bank account to manage your writing income and expenses. This helps keep your personal and business finances separate, making accounting and tax filing more straightforward.

- **Contracts and Agreements:**

   o   Always use contracts when working with editors, designers, or collaborators. These contracts should outline the scope of work, payment terms, and ownership rights. Consider consulting with a lawyer to draft standard contract templates for your business.

- **Insurance:**

   o   Depending on your activities, you might need business insurance. This could include liability insurance, especially if you're hosting events or working with clients, or errors and omissions insurance if you're providing services like editing or consulting.

A Little Betsy Note

Congratulations! You made it to the end of this book, and I have no doubt you'll tackle your writing and publishing journey with the same enthusiasm and determination! I know it might seem a bit overwhelming right now, but remember—take it one step at a time, and you'll get there. Sure, it's going to require some time and commitment, and there will be moments when you feel like tossing in the towel. But don't! Take a break, have a laugh with your writing buddies, and keep going.

Most importantly, make sure to have fun and enjoy every part of this adventure. What you're doing is truly amazing, and it's also incredibly rewarding. Don't worry if things don't always go according to plan. Stay calm, keep your eyes on the goals you set, and trust that everything will come together in its own perfect way.

Remember, many of the most successful writers heard "no" far more often than "yes" on their path to success. But it only takes one magical "yes" to change everything!

And when that glorious publication day finally arrives, celebrate like there's no tomorrow! You set out to do something incredible, and you did it—that deserves all the confetti and more!

Don't stress too much about the sales numbers. Sure, it's fantastic if your book flies off the shelves, but even if just one person reads it and feels a little more joyful, healed, or inspired, you've made a beautiful difference in the world.

Have questions? Looking for a writing coach or mastermind group? I am here to help. Visit my website at www.betsychasse.net to get in touch and learn about my programs to support writers like you!

XoB

Appendices

Writing Resources and Tools

In today's digital age, writers have access to a wealth of resources and tools that can enhance their writing process, help them stay organized, and support their publishing journey. Below is a curated list of some of the most useful resources and tools available for writers:

1. Writing and Editing Tools

- **Scrivener**: A powerful writing software designed specifically for long-form writing projects. It allows you to organize your manuscript, research, and notes all in one place.

- **Grammarly**: An AI-powered writing assistant that checks grammar, spelling, punctuation, and style. It's a valuable tool for self-editing before sending your work to an editor.

- **Hemingway App**: A tool that analyzes your writing for readability, highlighting complex sentences, passive voice, and other areas for improvement.

- **ProWritingAid:** A comprehensive editing tool that offers grammar checks, style suggestions, and detailed reports on your writing.

2. Productivity Tools

- **Trello**: A project management tool that helps you organize your writing tasks, set deadlines, and track progress. It's especially useful for managing multiple projects.

- **Evernote**: A note-taking app that allows you to capture ideas, organize research, and sync your notes across devices.

- **Focus@Will:** A music service that offers background music scientifically designed to improve focus and productivity, perfect for writing sessions.

3. Publishing and Formatting Tools

- **Vellum**: A professional formatting tool for creating beautifully formatted ebooks and print books. It's known for its user-friendly interface and high-quality output.

- **Reedsy Book Editor:** A free online tool that allows you to format your manuscript for publication, offering a simple interface and professional results.

- **Canva**: A graphic design tool that is easy to use for creating book covers, promotional materials, and social media graphics.

4. Research and Reference Resources

- **Google Scholar:** A free search engine for scholarly literature, providing access to academic papers, theses, books, and more.

- **JSTOR**: A digital library offering access to thousands of academic journals, books, and primary sources.

- **Thesaurus.com:** An online thesaurus that helps you find synonyms and expand your vocabulary.

Sample Query Letters and Book Proposals

Navigating the traditional publishing process often begins with crafting a compelling query letter and a strong book proposal. Below are examples to guide you through this essential part of your writing journey.

Sample Query Letter:

[Your Name]

[Your Address]

[City, State, ZIP Code]

[Email Address]

[Phone Number]

[Date]

[Agent's Name]

[Agency Name]

[Agency Address]

[City, State, ZIP Code]

Dear [Agent's Name],

I am seeking representation for my [genre] novel, [Title of Your Book], complete at [word count]. Given your interest in [specific genre or similar works the agent represents], I believe it would be a great fit for your list.

[Brief synopsis of your book – include the main plot, key characters, and what makes your book unique. Aim for 1-2 paragraphs.]

I am an [optional: mention relevant writing credentials, awards, or experience]. The full manuscript is available upon request. Thank you for considering [Title of Your Book]. I look forward to the possibility of working together.

Sincerely,

[Your Name]

Sample Non-Fiction Book Proposal:

Title Page:

Title of Your Book

Subtitle (if applicable)

By [Your Name]

[Contact Information]

The Writer's Room

Here's an example based on the Children's Book Outline:

[Your Name]

[Your Address]

[City, State, ZIP Code]

[Email Address]

[Phone Number]

[Date]

[Agent's Name]

[Agency Name]

[Agency Address]

[City, State, ZIP Code]

Dear [Agent's Name],

I am seeking representation for my 500-word children's picture book, Annie the Brave. Given your passion for heartwarming and imaginative children's stories, I believe it would be a wonderful addition to your list.

Annie the Brave is the tender story of a little ant named Annie who sets off on a journey to find her missing mother in the vast and bustling ant colony. Along the way, she encounters new friends like a wise old beetle, a timid caterpillar, and a grumpy snail, who all help her navigate the world above and below the ground. Through her adventures, Annie learns about courage, kindness, and the true meaning of family.

This story is intended for children ages 4 to 7 and combines whimsical illustrations with an emotionally resonant narrative that encourages empathy and resilience. Annie the Brave offers a gentle way to address the themes of loss and hope, making it both a comforting bedtime story and a tool for caregivers to discuss difficult topics.

I am a member of the Society of Children's Book Writers and Illustrators (SCBWI) and have had short stories published in children's magazines such as Highlights for Children. As a former elementary school teacher, I have spent years crafting stories that engage young minds and foster emotional growth.

The full manuscript is available upon request. Thank you for considering Annie the Brave. I look forward to the possibility of working together and bringing Annie's story to life for children and families everywhere.

Sincerely,

[Your Name]

Book Proposal:

Overview:

Provide a brief description of the book's subject, purpose, and target audience. Explain why this book is timely and important and why you are the right person to write it.

Market Analysis:

Describe the target market for your book. Include information about the size and demographics of the audience and why there is a demand for your book. Discuss competing titles and explain how your book will stand out.

Author Bio:

Highlight your qualifications, experience, and any platforms you have that would contribute to the marketing and promotion of the book.

Chapter Outline:

Provide a detailed outline of the book's structure. Include the title and a brief description of each chapter.

Sample Chapters:

Include one or two sample chapters that showcase your writing style and the quality of the content.

Marketing and Promotion Plan:

Outline your plan for promoting the book. Include any existing networks, speaking engagements, social media presence, or other marketing avenues you plan to utilize.

Here is an example book proposal: I suggest adding an image of yourself and any cover art or ideas for cover art or illustrations:

Book Proposal: Annie the Brave by [Your Name]

Title:

Annie the Brave

Author:

[Your Name]

Overview:

Annie the Brave is a heartwarming children's picture book that tells the story of Annie, a young ant who embarks on a journey to find her missing mother in a vast and bustling ant colony. Along the way, Annie meets a wise old beetle, a timid caterpillar, and a grumpy snail, each of whom helps her navigate the challenging and unfamiliar world above and below ground. Through her adventures, Annie learns about courage, kindness, and the true meaning of family.

Intended for children ages 4 to 7, this 500-word story combines whimsical illustrations with an emotionally resonant narrative. It offers a gentle way to address themes of loss, hope, and resilience, making it both a comforting bedtime story and a valuable tool for caregivers to discuss difficult topics with young children.

Target Audience:

- **Primary Audience:** Children ages 4 to 7
- **Secondary Audience:** Parents, caregivers, educators, librarians, and child psychologists looking for engaging, emotionally supportive stories that address the themes of loss, resilience, and the importance of family.

Market Analysis:

There is a growing demand for children's literature that addresses emotional and social challenges in a sensitive and age-appropriate manner. Books that help children navigate complex feelings and situations, like The Invisible String by Patrice Karst and The Rabbit Listened by Cori Doerrfeld, have been well-received and continue to be popular with parents and educators alike.

Annie the Brave fills a gap in the market for picture books that explore the themes of loss and resilience from a child-friendly perspective. The story's combination of imaginative adventure and emotional depth will appeal to both children and adults who seek meaningful, engaging stories that foster empathy and understanding.

Comparative Titles:

1. **The Invisible String by Patrice Karst** – A comforting story about the invisible bonds that connect us to the ones we love, even when they are far away.

2. **The Rabbit Listened by Cori Doerrfeld** – A gentle story about dealing with loss and finding comfort in understanding friends.

3. **Ida, Always by Caron Levis and Charles Santoso** – A story that helps children understand loss and the beauty of lasting memories.

Author Bio:

[Your Name] is a member of the Society of Children's Book Writers and Illustrators (SCBWI) and a former elementary school teacher with over ten years of experience engaging young minds through storytelling. [Your Name] has published short stories in Highlights for Children and is passionate about creating stories that nurture emotional intelligence, empathy, and resilience in young readers.

Chapter Outline / Book Breakdown:

Since Annie the Brave is a picture book, it follows a single, continuous narrative with the following story elements:

1. **Introduction:** Annie, a young ant, realizes her mother is missing in the busy ant colony. Feeling worried, she decides to embark on a journey to find her.

2. **First Encounter:** Annie meets a wise old beetle who teaches her to observe and listen to her surroundings to find clues.

3. **Second Encounter:** She meets a timid caterpillar who shares his fear of the unknown, encouraging Annie to face her own fears with bravery.

4. **Third Encounter:** Annie encounters a grumpy snail who teaches her patience and kindness in the face of adversity.

5. **Resolution**: After learning from her new friends, Annie finds her mother safe and sound. She learns that love and courage can guide her through any challenge.

6. **Conclusion**: Annie returns home with newfound confidence, realizing that she is never truly alone when surrounded by friends and family who care.

Illustration Style:

The illustrations will feature vibrant, whimsical art that captures the rich and diverse world of an ant colony. Each character Annie meets will have a distinct look and personality, reflecting their unique role in the story. The illustrations will be colorful and engaging, with a touch of humor to keep young readers entertained.

Marketing and Promotion Plan:

- **Social Media Campaigns:** Use Instagram and Facebook to share illustrations, character introductions, and behind-the-scenes looks at the creation of the book.

- **Partnerships with Child Psychologists and Educators:** Collaborate with professionals specializing in child development and emotional resilience to promote the book as a tool for discussing difficult emotions.

- **School and Library Events:** Organize book readings, workshops, and activities in schools and libraries to engage directly with the target audience.

- **Book Bloggers and Reviewers:** Reach out to children's book bloggers, reviewers, and influencers to build early buzz and generate reviews.

- **Virtual Book Launch:** Host a virtual book launch event with activities, Q&A, and giveaways to generate excitement and reach a broad audience.

Sample Text:

The pages below are samples from the story's text, showcasing the whimsical language, engaging dialogue, and heartwarming narrative style that defines Annie's journey.

[Include 1-2 sample pages of text]

Author Platform:

- Website and Blog: [Your Name] maintains a website and blog dedicated to children's literature, parenting tips, and early childhood education.

- Social Media Presence: Active on Instagram, Twitter, and Facebook, with a following of parents, educators, and children's literature enthusiasts.

- Public Speaking and Events: Experience speaking at educational workshops and community events focused on storytelling and child development.

*Depending on your book – Add up to 3 chapters or a writing sample.

Recommended Reading List

Developing as a writer requires constant learning and exposure to a variety of writing styles, techniques, and industry insights. Here is a list of recommended books that every writer should consider reading:

Books on the Craft of Writing:

- "On Writing: A Memoir of the Craft" by Stephen King: Part memoir, part master class, King's book offers valuable advice on writing and the writer's life.

- "Bird by Bird: Some Instructions on Writing and Life" by Anne Lamott: A candid and humorous guide to writing, offering practical advice and insights into the creative process.

- "The Elements of Style" by William Strunk Jr. and E.B. White: A classic guide to clear and concise writing, focusing on style, grammar, and usage.

- "Writing Down the Bones: Freeing the Writer Within" by Natalie Goldberg: A book that combines writing exercises with meditations on the creative process, encouraging writers to find their voice.

Books on Editing and Revision:

- "Self-Editing for Fiction Writers" by Renni Browne and Dave King: A comprehensive guide to revising and editing your own work, with tips on dialogue, point of view, and pacing.

- "The Artful Edit: On the Practice of Editing Yourself" by Susan Bell: A detailed look at the editing process, offering practical advice and techniques for self-editing.

Books on Publishing and the Writing Business:

- "The Business of Being a Writer" by Jane Friedman: An essential guide to the business side of writing, covering everything from publishing contracts to marketing and building a writing career.

- "How to Market a Book" by Joanna Penn: A comprehensive guide to marketing your book, with strategies for both traditional and self-publishing.

Inspiration and Writing Life:

- "Big Magic: Creative Living Beyond Fear" by Elizabeth Gilbert: A book about embracing creativity, overcoming fear, and living a fulfilling creative life.

- "The War of Art: Break Through the Blocks and Win Your Inner Creative Battles" by Steven Pressfield: A motivational guide to overcoming resistance and staying productive as a writer.

As I mentioned earlier, I developed the process outlined in this book over many years of writing books as well as for films and documentaries. I have read many books, essays, and publications and researched best practices, etc.

This isn't the "right way"; it's my way.

Below is a list of references that I have used over the years:

1. **Writing Craft and Techniques:**
   - King, S. (2000). On Writing: A Memoir of the Craft. Scribner.
   - Lamott, A. (1994). Bird by Bird: Some Instructions on Writing and Life. Anchor Books.
   - Strunk, W., Jr., & White, E. B. (1999). The Elements of Style (4th ed.). Longman.
   - Goldberg, N. (2005). Writing Down the Bones: Freeing the Writer Within. Shambhala Publications.
   - Bell, J. S. (2008). Plot & Structure: Techniques and Exercises for Crafting a Plot That Grips Readers from Start to Finish. Writer's Digest Books.

2. **Overcoming Writer's Block:**
   - Cameron, J. (2002). The Artist's Way: A Spiritual Path to Higher Creativity. TarcherPerigee.
   - Ueland, B. (1987). If You Want to Write: A Book About Art, Independence, and Spirit. Graywolf Press.
   - Pressfield, S. (2002). The War of Art: Break Through the Blocks and Win Your Inner Creative Battles. Black Irish Entertainment LLC.

3. **Editing and Revising:**
   - Browne, R., & King, D. (2004). Self-Editing for Fiction Writers: How to Edit Yourself into Print (2nd ed.). HarperCollins.
   - Clark, R. P. (2008). The Glamour of Grammar: A Guide to the Magic and Mystery of Practical English. Little, Brown, and Company.
   - Bell, S. (2007). The Artful Edit: On the Practice of Editing Yourself. W. W. Norton & Company.

4. **Preparing Your Manuscript for Submission:**

    o   Friedman, J. (2018). The Business of Being a Writer. University of Chicago Press.

    o   Larsen, M., & Pomada, E. (2003). The Writer's Guide to Book Editors, Publishers, and Literary Agents. The Writer.

5. **Traditional Publishing:**

    o   Curtis, R. (2003). How to Get Your Book Published. Houghton Mifflin Harcourt.

    o   Maas, D. (2001). The Career Novelist: A Literary Agent Offers Strategies for Success. Writer's Digest Books.

    o   Dystel, J., & Goderich, M. (2013). How to Write a Great Query Letter. Dystel & Goderich Literary Management.

6. **Working with a Publisher:**

    o   Shatzkin, M., & Riger, R. (2012). The Book Business: What Everyone Needs to Know. Oxford University Press.

    o   Zuckerman, A., & Jewell, W. (2003). How to Get Happily Published (5th ed.). HarperPerennial.

7. **Self-Publishing:**

    o   Penn, J. (2018). How to Market a Book. Curl Up Press.

    o   Gaughran, D. (2018). Let's Get Digital: How to Self-Publish, and Why You Should. David Gaughran.

    o   Hocking, A. (2012). The Self-Publishing Guide. St. Martin's Griffin.

8. **Marketing Your Self-Published Book:**

    o   Penn, J. (2014). How to Market a Book. Curl Up Press.

    o   Fox, J. (2016). Your First 1,000 Copies: The Step-by-Step Guide to Marketing Your Book. Archangel Ink.

9. **Distribution and Sales:**

    o   Reidy, D. (2015). A Simple Guide to Self-Publishing. BookBaby.

    o   Handley, A., & Chapman, C. C. (2010). Content Rules: How to Create Killer Blogs, Podcasts, Videos, eBooks, Webinars (and More) That Engage Customers and Ignite Your Business. Wiley.

10. Legal and Financial Considerations:

- Walker, J. (2011). Self-Employed Tax Solutions: Simple Ways to Avoid IRS Troubles and Save Money. CreateSpace Independent Publishing Platform.

- Sakaduski, N. (2014). Taxes for Writers. Mansion Field.

- Pressfield, S. (2011). Do the Work. Black Irish Entertainment LLC.

11. Building a Writing Career:

- Coyne, J. (2015). Starting Your Career as a Freelance Writer. Allworth Press.

- Robinson, J. (2016). Write, Publish, Repeat: The No-Luck-Required Guide to Self-Publishing Success. Sterling & Stone.

12. Staying Inspired and Evolving as a Writer:

- Gilbert, E. (2015). Big Magic: Creative Living Beyond Fear. Riverhead Books.

- DeSalvo, L. (1999). Writing as a Way of Healing: How Telling Our Stories Transforms Our Lives. Beacon Press.

13. Additional References:

- U.S. Copyright Office. (n.d.). Copyright registration. Retrieved from https://www.copyright.gov/registration/

- United States Patent and Trademark Office (USPTO). (n.d.). Trademark basics: What every small business should know now, not later. Retrieved from https://www.uspto.gov/trademarks/basics

- Internal Revenue Service (IRS). (n.d.). Self-employed individuals tax center. Retrieved from https://www.irs.gov/businesses/small-businesses-self-employed/self-employed-individuals-tax-center

- U.S. Small Business Administration (SBA). (n.d.). Choose a business structure. Retrieved from https://www.sba.gov/business-guide/launch-your-business/choose-business-structure

www.ingramcontent.com/pod-product-compliance
Lightning Source LLC
Chambersburg PA
CBHW042358030426
42337CB00032B/5143